Beneath T

By. ~~Tracy~~

North-Star Publishing
2003 copyright
P.O. Box 4502
Prairie View, Texas 77446

Cover Designed by Countryside Photography
1-800-404-3288
Waller, Texas

Acknowledgements:

To my beautiful wife who stood beside me and understood the pains, anguish and frustrations of having to edit, edit and re-edit. Thanks for allowing me to burn the night-lights to see this book become a reality.

To all of my students from Reed Avenue Elementary, Lincoln Elementary and Prairie View A&M University keep the faith. A special thank you to the faithful three + one at Prairie View University, Michalle Wiggins, Nakesha Francis, Jeanine Davis, and Marcus Green ------ who helped me edit my book when it was in its final stages.

Dedication:

This book is dedicated to the memory of my father the late Warren Andrus Sr. and my brother Michael James Andrus. This book is also dedicated to all of my brothers and sisters who taught me most of what I know.

This book is dedicated to my mother who is the greatest woman that I know and certainly my hero.

Last but not least this book is dedicated to all of my brothers and sisters who are still catching hell in America. A special shout out and much love to all of my brothers and sisters locked up in jails and prisons all over the United States especially, the brothers at Wade Correctional Center in Homer, La.

Special love and dedication to all students seeking knowledge all over the world.

"We will never be free until we are heard and there will never be peace until we get our piece".

Tracy Andrus, 2003

We Wear the Mask

We wear the mask that grins and lies, It hides our cheeks and
Shades our eyes, -- This debt we pay to human guile; with torn
And bleeding hearts we smile, and mouth with myriad
subtleties.

Whys should the world be over wise, in counting all our tears?
And sighs? Nay let them only see us, while we wear the mask.

We smile, but, O great Christ, our cries to thee from tortured
Souls arise. We sing, but oh the clay is vile beneath our feet,
And long the mile; But let the world dream otherwise, we wear
The mask!

Paul Lawrence Dunbar

Beneath The Skin Of Black Folks
By: Tracy Andrus

Introduction

This book focuses on the experiences that I have encountered as a black man living in America. In this book I speak not only of my experiences but the experiences of millions of black folk in America who may never have the opportunity to tell white folks how they really feel. I do not speak for all black folks. There are some black folks in America who have made two dollars over rent and no longer understand the struggles that the masses of black folk encounter day to day. These black folks do not wish to be identified with their brothers and sisters who strive to survive daily. The brothers and sisters that I speak about in this book live everyday of their life on the brink of disaster.

In this book I lift the veil again exactly 100 years after the publishing of W.E.B. Dubois's The Souls Of Black Folks to give white folks in America a true glimpse of how Black Folks in America Really feel. The matters and issues that are discussed in this book will not go away. These issues are very real and continue to divide America and Americans. Until black folk and white folk sit down face to face and resolve the issues of race and racism this nation will never rise to its fullest potential. Racism, prejudice, and discrimination are as

American as apple pie. These factors have constantly impeded our progress as a nation. This book deals with race at its core. The intent and purpose of this book is not to offend or divide but to bind up and heal wounds.

We live in a country that values aviation, star wars, technology, space travel, war, politics, capitalism and dominance over other countries more than she does African Americans whose fore-parents toiled from "cant to cant". ("Many slaves could not see in the morning when they left home for work in the cotton fields and many worked in the fields until they could not see in the evening when they returned home). These slaves helped to created the massive stockpiles of wealth that has made America the super-power that she is today. Yet many black folk in America are entrapped in an airtight cage of poverty.

Black folk are constantly told by republicans and conservatives that there are no more free lunches at the table and that everyone has to pull themselves up by their own bootstraps. I pause at this moment for millions of impoverished black folks to say to white folks that many of my brothers and sisters cannot pull themselves up by their bootstraps because they don't have boots!

Black folks are still waiting to be paid in America. Many people believe that reparations are handouts but if white folks took the profits of slaves without exerting efforts to till the ground and heaped up fortunes making cotton king in the south why should black folks feel that they are receiving a handout? We are only claiming what is our. If America can spend 100 billion dollars a year to keep the masses of black folk incarcerated, I know she can spend 100 billion in reparations to help keep black folk out of prisons and jails.

Beneath The Skin of Black Folks deals with the everyday struggles of millions of black men and women who have lived with the pains and anguish of just being black in America.

In this book I spare no words. I do not ask for forgiveness and I make no apologies. I am only interested in telling the truth. At this point APA is not important. I am more interested in conveying my thoughts and points. If you as the reader read this book and understand what I am saying, I would have accomplished my objective. We must begin to question things as a race of people. We should not accept everything we read as being etched in stone. As soon as we learn the game they change the rules.

The sooner black folks and white folks come to grips with our true feelings with each other the sooner we will be able to deal with the problems that continuously impede our progress as a nation.

When Du Bois published The Souls of Black Folks on April 18, 1903 he said, "the problem of the twentieth century was the color-line". Today in 2003, I say that the problem of the twenty-first century is still the problem of the color line.

Racism in America has not subsided but in many respects has intensified. Today we deal with a new subtle type of racism that is most cruel. During the turn of the century white folks who did not like you showed you that they did not like you. Today in America many white folks do not tell black folk that they do not like us but they create barriers and laws that show us that they do not like black folk as a people.

I must also make clear in this book that not all white folks are bad and not all black folks are good. It is not the intention of this book to heighten tension among the races, but to create dialog so that we may sit down and gather understanding.

Just like a wife and husband must communicate each other's feelings to maintain a healthy relationship so must races. If we continue to ignore each other's feelings we will continue to have race riots and protest all over America. As I write today February 4, 2003 the Klu Klux Klan is planning a rally march in New Mexico.

We can no longer sweep our feelings under the rug. In reading this book the reader is allowed to glimpse into the world of black folks and see how black folks in America really feel and see what really lies beneath the skin of black folks.

Being Black In America

If you are black in America, I don't care if you are rich or poor, whether you live in a million dollar house or a shack, whether you are a governor or a brain surgeon. It does not matter if you sit on the Supreme Court or if you or the Chief of Security for the President. To many white folks even most of your peers, you are still a nigger. White folks may divide you into a certain class and treat you with somewhat more dignity but in most of their minds you are still a nigger. White folks normally view you as one of the following; a rich nigger, a poor nigger, a good Uncle Tom Nigger, a Uppity nigger or a (troublesome-stirring - up-trouble) Nigger and when you drop the adjectives you are still a Nigger in the eyesight of these white folks.

Release

Beneath The Skin Of Black Folks is a release of anguish, pain, suffering, frustration, and tension that black folks have endured for countless generations in America.

Paul Lawrence Dunbar illustrated so beautifully in his poem *We wear the mask, how* black folks have always had to smile in order not to offend white folks. Many black folks have smiled pretending to be happy, gracious and appreciative because that is what was expected of them. That was the status quo of the day used to appease their masters, employers and associates. In the hearts of these black folks they knew that their smiles were farthest from the truth.

Why I speak for Black Folks

In this book, I speak for all African Americans who cannot say what they want to say because they are afraid that they may be fired from their jobs, laid off, blackballed, retaliated against, demoted etc. Beneath the skin of black folks go beneath the skin and tell the story of how black folks really feel without

10

worrying about the repercussions. This book goes beneath the smiles, hand shaking, head scratching, Uncle Toming of blacks and express how the majority of black folks in America really feel.

There is one thing for certain that the white man will never know and that is how it feels to be black. White folks can do all of the research they want, but they will never know how it really feels to be black in America. Many black folks in America catch hell from the man everyday.

Purpose of The Book

The purpose of this book is to express the feeling of black folks all over America. I speak for the rich and poor, employed and unemployed, incarcerated and free, protestant and catholic etc. I speak for every African American in America who is catching hell from the white man. It is my hope that we will be able to use this book as a starting point to deal with the many racial problems that we face from day to day in America. We can no longer be fooled and we can no longer afford to ignore the biggest problem in American civilization and that is the problem of racism.

Black folks are intelligent enough to make rules for themselves, yet white folks make all of the laws and rules in America and expect us to follow them like little lambs. Today is the beginning of the dawning of a new era among black folks. Black folk must come together and vote for one another and support one another. We must register to vote. We must vote. The voting ballot is our ticket to getting what is rightfully our. Let's not talk about it in 2003 but let's be about it. Register and vote.

This book exposes the myths and realities of racism in our everyday lives. Black folks must recognize that it does not matter if you are a Board Member or CEO of a Fortune 500 Company, a Professor, Preacher, common laborer, Policeman etc. when you are out of the presence of most white men you are still just another nigger.

Let us not be fooled, I know that I will be called a racist and many other names for writing this book, but that's okay! I hope that this book live throughout eternity or until racism no longer exist in this world.

White folks are quick to say that blacks pull the race card. This may be true considering the fact that blacks must live day in and day out at tiptoe stance never really knowing what will happen at the next moment in life.

Are blacks aggressive? Are blacks apprehensive? Of course we are, this is what white folks have caused us to evolve into.

It really makes my stomach turn to see white folks act like blacks are over-reacting about the race card when they know dam well in their hearts that they really don't want to have anything to do with the black man.

Many whites will move in the woods (suburbs) to get away from blacks. Whites when looking for homes look for homes in

12

white neighborhoods. Black folks on the other hand will gladly move into a white neighborhood. When was the last time you witnessed a middleclass white family move into an exclusively black housing subdivision when there were white subdivisions around?

Net Worth

White folks have always felt that they were more than black folks and that is one of the reasons why they have not wanted to be around black folks. Many white folks do not want their children around blacks because they feel that blacks are inferior, lazy, dumb, stupid, love sex, have kids out of wedlock, immoral, don't maintain their property, want something for nothing etc.

Most white folks are interested in one thing and that is to get as much as they can and they don't give a dam who they have to hurt, maim or kill to accomplish their objective. Before you say that this statement is cruel think about the history of the white man in America.

This book also details how black folks in America view White Society, The American Justice System and the white folks who control these systems. This book also reveals how white Americans in the past; present and future have conspired to keep black folks in America down and out.

Common Sense

Every black person in his or her right mind should be able to see that there is and has always been in place a conspiracy in America to use and destroy black folks. This conspiracy is carried on even unto this day. Beneath the skin of black folks reflects upon the ways in which the welfare system, drugs, guns, crime, racism, prejudice, laws, poverty, religion, and gangs are used to perpetuate a lifestyle of dependency for blacks in general.

When we as black folks open our eyes we will realize that white folks in American society allow certain amounts of drug trafficking, gun smuggling, murders, welfare dependents, homelessness, sickness etc. to keep the system operating at its "business as usual" capacity.

My Beliefs And Ideologies About Race And Racism 2003

I want to make it clear that I make no apologies for my work neither do I wear a mask when explaining the real state of black America and the way that the majority of blacks really feel living in America. If it somehow seems in this book that I am blaming white folks for most of the problems of black people than "you've got it"! You are correct! Realistically, it is time that we face the plain truth if we are to move on in this new millennium. I believe that open rebuke is better than secret love. Had white folks never transported black folks to America to work in their fields and wait on them in serfdom black folks

14

would not be in the shape that we are in today. White folks must confess that they have exploited black folks at all cost. White folks are responsible for separating the black family and permanently scaring the black race in America for generations to come.

The Big Lie

Black folks did not buy a ticket to come to America; neither did they volunteer to leave their homelands in Africa. White folk have tried to sell black folk that story about other blacks capturing Africans and selling them into slavery to the Europeans for goods and merchandise for a long time, yet we know better.

If black folk did sell other Africans it was certainly on a small scale. Once again we cannot be quick to believe everything that white folks tell us or put in our books. Anyone can speak or tell a lie.

If anything such as this took place, there had to have been an initiation on the part of white folks. Black folks once again we must not jump to believing all that we read. Personally, I do not believe that Africans just waited at the dock for a European ship to pass by, flag them down and ask them if they wanted to buy some slaves. If we think about this realistically and study the facts we would know better. White Europeans came into Africa long ago with the bible preaching salvation. They told Africans to trust in God. Africans were told that the God that they were serving was the wrong God.

It is a documented fact that Sir David Livingston went into Africa with his bible preaching about Jesus and the plan of salvation and when he departed sometimes later, the Africans were holding on to the bible and Livingston had the deeds to all of their land. What trickery in the master's name! We can argue all we want but we must come to understand the truth about the black man in America. Had it not been for greed, wickedness and the exploitation by the white man black folks would not be in the shape that they are in today in America.

Born Black In America

Being black in America means more than just residing beneath the black skin that we inherited from our birth. Being black in America in 2003 is bittersweet. It's a sobering experience in which we are forced to deal with from day to day. Being black in America means that the good that you do is never really good enough. Black folks in America must possess extraordinary talent to achieve relative success and grandeur in American culture.

Therefore, I make it plain that it is no coincidence that I decided to pursue my Doctorate Degree in Juvenile Justice. I have been told numerous times by my professors that a master's degree would suffice for a teaching position in college because colleges needed more black instructors and professors. Yet, I know that if I am to compete with white folks, I must possess something greater than the ordinary.

I have read during my college years numerous books and articles on how whites have gone into black neighborhoods and lived with black families to see how it felt to be black and how black people survived, but the truth again that whites will never feel what black people feel unless they can somehow become black!

Racist Teachers (How we Teach Racism in 2003)

While it is true that the gaps of racism and prejudice has been somewhat reduced in the last forty years, the fact still remains that there are many blacks and whites who are still teaching racism and prejudice to their children. Some people teach racism to their children knowingly and others unknowingly.

Every time a parent tell their child that they cannot invite a certain friend to their home because that friend is black or white that parent is teaching racism. Every time a parent tell their kid that they cannot date a certain person because of the color of that person's skin or their ethnic background that parent is teaching racism. Every time an employer tell a human resources personnel manager not to hire someone because of their skin color, or ethnicity he or she is practicing prejudice and racism.

When black folks attend white folks churches and white folks tell black folks that God loves them and yet they are advised to attend the church down the street where there are more blacks

17

they are practicing and teaching racism in the name of the Lord. When you put your house up for sale because a black couple just purchases the house next door you are teaching your children and practicing racism. If white folks or black folks move from their comfortable homes just to avoid having neighbors of different ethnicities or race then we are teaching racism.

Black folks are well aware of the fact that racism is alive and well in the U.S. Blacks must come to realize that unless we do something to help ourselves and the generations that will follow nothing significant will ever be done by the white man to improve our conditions.

That is why black folks must continue to travel from state to state urging our black churches and black leaders to pull together and form coalitions that can dismantle the barriers that have so long existed in oppressing African Americans.

While living in Shreveport, I had the privilege to work with a young lady whose father was a very prominent pastor in Shreveport. Her father had a very large congregation. She said to me that she and her father did not get alone very well because her father taught in his church that black folks and white folks should not date, commingle or marry one another. He taught that they should not have children with one another. She said that her father used the scripture that god used with Solomon when he told Solomon to stay away from the bedlamites

18

because they would turn his heart away from God to solidify his beliefs that the races were to remain separate.

I still believe that many pastors are preaching this same gospel today. Caucasian Pastors will tell you in a minute God did not mean for black folks and white folks to be with one another intimately!

How can we preach that God is not a respecter of persons on one hand yet we don't like one another because of the color of each other's skin? Black folks and white folks shout, receive the Holy Ghost and speak in tongues and outside of the church we can't speak to one another.

I am an optimist and believe that the relationship between black folks and white folks are improving. As the older generations of racists and undercover Klansmen of yesterday die out, the new generations of white folks and black folks who have had the opportunity to attend public schools and colleges together will realize that some of the things that they have heard from their parents about black folks are simply not true.

I've heard many myths about black people from white people including the myth that black people are dumb, lazy, confrontational, will steal and must be watched, they can never be trusted, always looking for a handout, not aggressive, biologically inferior, criminals, evil, no good, have large penis, have a tail, make love like animals etc.

The younger generation of blacks and whites will be responsible for changing these myths. It is not my intentions to infer that all older white folks are racist, bad or prejudice because that would be the farthest from the truth. However, I am saying that the majority of white folks that do not like black folks and prefer that blacks not commingle or be integrated into white culture are those pre civil rights era born white folks who embellished life as it was in what they refer to as "The Good Ole Days".

I think that it is important to pause her and reiterate to the readers of this book that despite the harshness of this book, I am no racist.

I am a realist and believe that black folks and white folks can only be set free if they know the truth and speak the truth. Like the short story of James Joyce, *"The Passing Of Grandson"*, sometimes we don't know the truth until its too late. If the slave owner in this short story would have known that Grandison was not pleased living on his plantation he would have never allowed Grandison to travel to the border of Canada, where he could escape to freedom. The story of Grandison is the story of millions of black folks today who work, smile and pretend to be happy, while waiting for the opportunity to break free and enjoy real true freedom.

Whether we admit it or not, we do wear the mask that smiles and grin but beneath the skin, oh what anguish, what pain oh wicked man that I am who shall deliver me from the body of this death, for with my mind I serve the law of God, yet with my flesh the law of sin.

Admiration of Black Leaders

I have always admired certain leaders since my youth. When I was in Jr. high school I became fascinated with the thoughts of complete freedom. Complete freedom to me is the kind of freedom where everything is equal. With this kind of freedom everyone would have the same chance to achieve goals. This is not an illusionary freedom. This kind of freedom allow black folks and white folks to be treated the same.

Martin King, Malcolm X, Nelson Mandela, Marcus Garvey, Jesse Jackson, Louis Farrakhan, Tupac Shakur, Rev. Al Sharpton, Tom Joyner, Tavis Smiley, Bill Cosby, Richard Pryor, Bernie Mac, Ice Cube, Ice T, Spike Lee, Mike Tyson, Muhammad Ali, George Foremen, Will Smith, Jada Pinkett, Denzel Washington, Halle Berry, Oprah, Mike Jordan, Shaq, B.I.G., Shan John, Michael Jackson, O.J., John Singleton, and millions of other brothers and sisters have been and still is my role models.

Marion Berry and others who have fought for the rights of the underclass have been the kinds of people that I have learned to love with special passion.

I have always believed and still believe that God will one day allow me to be put in a position to help poor people. My prayer has always been that God would let me speak for those people who are not able to speak for themselves.

I have also always admired the writings and lives of Karl Marx, Diogenes, Henry David Thoreau, Gandhi and Socrates for their resistance and resilience.

The First Terrorists On North American Soil

White folks and black folks are scared to fly today because of 911. On September 11, 2001 terrorist high jacked several planes and crashed them into the world trade center and the pentagon. That was a terrible tragedy. Many innocent lives were lost. One plane was headed for the white house but never made it.

As a result of 911 white folks have revitalized and revolutionized security in every airport in America. It is very clear that white folks are afraid of the terrorists. Since 911 Arabs and middle easterners have become public enemy number one. One of my colleagues in the PhD program (Fred Ford) said that the hyphen dropped after 911 and African Americans became Americans. After this tragedy black folks were not viewed as public enemy number one. The terrorists accomplished their objective of disrupting the American economy.

Terrorists did not stop black folk from flying. Most black folks that I know have always been afraid to fly. Many black folks will tell you in a minute that if God meant for them to fly he would have given them wings. That is a polite way of them saying don't even think about it because they are not flying.

The only terrorist that I see is President Bush. Black folks and white folks are scared. We are buying duct tape and plastic trying to brace ourselves for nuclear war. People all over the world is marching and protesting against a war yet America is set on fighting. Is having oil that important? Is having oil worth the millions of lives that will be affected by war? It is very eerie to think about what the flag and the golden rule means and then look at what we are doing to others.

We have conflicting values in America. We wonder why children are so mixed up. We hear the government say that killing is wrong and then see them execute criminals. Our children hear their parents, teachers, pastor and president say that they are Christians and that we should love one another and then the president orders a bomb dropped on a whole country because we need some oil.

If the Bush Administration proceeds with this war they will be guilty of "Oil Jacking". When black folks take folks cars by force they are guilty of "car jacking" so the president and his staff should be held to the same standards.

America is a superpower but when power is abused, God has a way of intervening and letting abusers know who really has all power and who is almighty.

Reap what we sow

The bible says that we reap what we sow. The white man was the first terrorist on North American soil. The white man terrorized the Indians and then he terrorized the African

23

American, and the Hispanics and any other race that threatened his economic or political power in any way.

There are so many horror stories that can be told about white folks in America. Indians were stripped of their land and placed on reservations with blankets laced with polio. White folks wanted to eradicate the Native Americans.

Slaves caught and are still catching hell from white folks in America. White folks really have some nerves telling black folks to respect the constitution and salute the American flag! The constitution was not written for black folks that are evident from just looking at the preamble.

When black folks decided that they were going to vote after the civil war Klansmen decided that they would put some fear in the hearts of black folks. Klansmen burned houses and lynched by any means necessary, any Negro who dared go to the voting booth or even spoke about wanting to exercise his right to vote.

Spooked!

The white man has terrorized black folks for centuries. Today, they are still terrorizing black folks. When black folks see a police car trailing them they become terrorized and paranoid even when they know they have not did anything. When black folks exit stores in the mall or any shopping place they are terrorized when they walk out of the store because they think that the security loss prevention detector might go off. Black folk are scared even when they know they have not did anything wrong. White folks have black folks scared to do many things.

Black folk are paranoid. We know that the white man can be dirty. In the state of Louisiana white folks cut off the heads of 16 black folks and stuck there heads on poles along the banks of the Mississippi River to instill fear in others black folks after the signing of the Emancipation Proclamation.

Bin Laden

Black folks are not scared of Osama Bin Laden and I do not believe that Osama Bin Laden is scared of black folks. "If Osama Bin Laden had a choice he would probably blow up white folks in power and he would not touch black folks. Most of the Arabs that I have spoken to in the corner grocery stores hate white folks not black folks. They are very adamant about reducing the power of white folks. Why should they be afraid of black folks? When black folks see Wall Street, The White House, The senate, The Congress, The supreme Court, The Presidents and anything else that represent and resemble power in America they see white folks.

When foreigners burn American flags and protest against America in other countries they are not rallying against black folks they are rallying against white folks. I believe that if they could they would spare black folks because we have not did them anything.

Saddam 2003 and the approaching war

White folks must come to understand the real motives of black folks. Lets be real. Do you think that black folks join the military because they are patriotic and want to defend America? Of course not! Defend America for what! Why should black folks defend a country that still does not fully accept black folks? We have not melted in the melting pot! We are still visible. We are still black. Assimilation does not work with us. We are still the flies in the milk. We cannot hide! The Irish, German, French, Russians, Jews, Scandinavians and even the Hispanics can melt in the pot but the texture of our hair and the color of our skin will not allow us to melt and assimilate.

Most black folks join the military to have a stable source of income and a stable job. Why in the world would black folks fight to keep America free? America has not treated black folks right since we've been here. The Iraqis have not called black folks niggers. They have not opposed affirmative action. They have not practiced racism, prejudice and discrimination against the black man in America.

I know that America must keep Americans safe including black folks. That may not be by choice. Black folks are not enthralled to see Secretary Powell at the United Nations arguing that the United States must attack Iraq. That does not look good for black folks. We are creating enemies for ourselves. To the Iraqis it seem that black folks are running something here in America. Black folks don't run anything here in America. When you move Powell, Rice, and Thomas we can really see the picture clearly.

Black folks have much more power than we think. We can realize our power if we quit letting white folks hoodwink us. We want the same thing that they want. No more and no less and we will not stop striving for what is rightfully ours until we get it.

When we start talking about terrorists and terrorism in America we cannot forget the secret societies (Klan) of the 1860's that formed after the Civil War. The Klu Klux Klan was and still is the worst terrorist on American soil today. Today the Klan continues to terrorize little black boys and girls and carefully remove the African American breadwinners out of their homes. The absence of the black male from the home causes the black family to be in disarray but we don't talk about this kind of terror.

Nonviolence or Non-existence: Can't we all just get alone?

Rev. Dr. Martin Luther King stated long ago that we would either live with nonviolence or we would become non-existent. Today in America we are at the brink of war. Today as I sit before the television the future of America and world peace becomes more uncertain. North Korea has revealed that they have a nuclear warhead that can reach American soil. France, Russia, Germany, China and many of the other superpowers have refused to support the United States in this war that will take more foreign and domestic lives than both World War I and World War II combined.

27

The weapons of our warfare are different today. There are allies and enemies sitting by buttons twenty-four seven waiting for a directive. War today would kill millions of people. What are we fighting for? Will Saddam not disarm peacefully? Why should Saddam disarm?

Why can America built all of the weapons of mass destruction and refuse to let other countries do the same. Why should America be so privileged? White folks want to dominate the world and all black folks know that better than anybody else. It is a real shame that black folks who are soldiers will lose their lives defending a country where we are still not free from racism, prejudice and discrimination. Don't believe for one minute that most of the black folks fighting this war is fighting because they are patriotic and believe in American patriotism. Black folks join the military for job security. Not for patriotism.

Black folks don't wonder why Malcolm X, Huey Newton, Minister Louis Farrakhan, and a growing number of black clergy were and are mad as hell. We know why they felt and feel the way that they do.

Black folks will continue to die as they have in the Civil War, World War I, World War II, Vietnam War, Desert Storm and other small conflicts and when they return to America they will still be treated like second-class citizens. If America expects black folks to develop interest in the United States then there are some things that must change.

Black folks can no longer be treated like second-class citizens. We must be given the same opportunities as white folks. I discuss some of the things such as the subtle forms of racism, prejudice and discrimination in later chapters. These things must change if black folks are to change in America.

Do our children deserve to live under a cloud of destruction because American officials have decided to dominate to world? We must live in peace or we will suffer massive destruction. We can all live together.

Saddam has threatened to destroy all of the oil reserves in the Middle East if a war becomes imminent. If America wants oil we need to continue to buy oil. Today is December 13, 2003. Tomorrow is Valentine's Day and I hope that we don't have another Valentine's Day massacre. Non-violence or Nonexistence? That is the question.

Why Can't White Folk Get Over O.J?

Many white folks have still not accepted the verdict of Not Guilty. This case whether we want to admit it or not did not open old wounds. The wounds were never closed. This case and the verdict only agitated the wound. Many whites felt and still feel that O.J. should have had a date with the gas chamber, the electric chair "old Sparky" or the lethal injection gurney. When O. J. was acquitted that was a slap in the face to white folk. White folks just cannot get over O.J. This is one of the reasons that many whites cannot stop talking about it! O.J. knows that he must walk very lightly because many white folks are waiting for you to mess up.

White folks have been infuriated since the O.J. trial. I have been in many classes when O.J.'s name has surfaced and white folks just know beyond a doubt that O.J. killed Ron Goldman and Nicole Simpson. They will go to their deathbed believing that O.J. is guilty. After this verdict O.J.'s Heisman, his years at U.S.C. and Buffalo did not mean anything. On the day of the verdict O. J. became just another nigger in the sight of many white folks. Have you seen the juice on any commercials lately? He was acquitted so why didn't he resume his career? The answer is quite simple, most white folks hate O.J.

White folks should not be mad at O.J. If they want to be mad at anyone they should be mad at Mark Furman. Furman, in my opinion was too anxious. He did not follow procedure and as a result most of the evidence that he collected had to be suppressed.

In the 40's, 50's and 60's black folks words were very seldom if ever taken over white folks words. There was virtually no justice in the courtroom for black folks. When O.J. won Black Folks won. For the first time in American society a black man had been exonerated for killing a white man and a white woman. O.J. had proven that even though the odds are stacked against you. If you have the right money and a dream team of lawyers, money could get you off the hook.

Black folks in America know that if O.J. were poor he would be dead right now. Money changes things. O.J.'s case help to explain why black folks go to jail and white folks go home. Jeffery Reiman's title to his book is on the money. Reiman's book is entitled *"The rich get richer and the poor get prison"*. Most black folks don't have money to hire good lawyers. Poor black folks must accept indigent defender lawyers that really don't give a dam about them. Most indigent defender lawyers only know two words. Plea Bargain.

The O.J. verdict did not open a new wound among black folks and white folks. This verdict elicited a response that actually exposed how white folks felt all alone.

What White Folks Must Acknowledge And Accept Before We Can Make Progress In America

Many white folks born prior to 1960 have been exposed to the racism that black folks were forced to endure during the civil rights era. Most whites born during and prior to the Civil Rights era were accustomed to seeing prejudice and racism. Many of these white folks never threw a stone but they supported the evil deeds of other white folks.

White folks must acknowledge that slavery did exist and that it was horrible and that they owe black folks reparations. We never did get our forty acres and a mule. Had black folks received their forty acres and a mule their forthcoming

31

generations may not be in the positions that we are in. White folks created black folks.

Malcolm X article was entitled the hate that hate produces. When white folks hate black folks that produce a reciprocal hate. We cannot have peace until we get our piece. Reparations are due! I would propose that all blacks in America be given 100,000.00, which is a fraction of what the cost of forty acres and a mule would have cost with interest up to this day.

America's Conspiracy To Kill Niggers And Black Folks

Black folks are dying. We are being locked up. We are unemployed. We are stressing. We need help. America has built a superpower nation upon the backs of black folks. Now that automation and technology has replaced slave labor white folks are set on kicking black folks to the curb. We have become eyesores to many white folks. Therefore we have been shackled again and we have been put to work again for free. Slavery is not over! Look in your state constitution and you will find out that slavery is permitted in 2003 but only under one condition and that is when a man or woman is incarcerated. The Emancipation Proclamation was supposed to abolish slavery but did it really abolish slavery? If we don't wake up, speak up, stand up, get up, and step up to the plate face-to-face, eye-to-eye and demand our rights we are all doomed to die.

Black folks get the bad end of the stick on everything. We have high infant mortality rates, high cancer rates, high HIV rates, high blood pressure, high rates of sugar diabetes, high homicide rates, high poverty rates, high crime rates, high drop-out rates. I don't know if we are cursed or if we are being used as guinea pigs. Are white folks experimenting with us? Are doctors using black patients as laboratory mice? If white folks would put polio agents in the covers of the native American and inject syphilis in black folks in Alabama, and ship cocaine into black neighborhoods to see how addictive the drug is, I would not be surprised to find out that white doctors are injecting black patients with HIV. This would be a matter of eugenics (Population Control).

Black folks do not believe for one minute that it is just a coincidence that there are many guns, much dope, high unemployment, liquor stores, projects, and heavy police patrol in the black neighborhood.

White folks have always felt it necessary to keep black folks in check. White folks in the 1830's felt that black folks were to passive to rebel. White folks doing this time had the audacity to believe that black folks were happy and content. Other white folks felt that black folks were to dumb and stupid to put up any kind of fight.

White folks learned a hard and expensive lesson in 1837. During this year a young black preacher named Nat Turner said that he had a vision from God and he and a few other slaves killed his master and 51 other white plantation owners.

After this massacre whites forbid blacks to meet alone. They had to have escorts in church and at picnics. Blacks could no longer be trusted. The same thing is true today. It has always amazed me how white folks act like they are so concerned about black folks.

I have often wondered about what do white people really think about blacks. I looked at President Bush select Colin Powell and Condalezza Rice as part of his cabinet. President Bush made the statement that "if any Americans work hard this is the kind of reward that they can achieve".

I think that this kind of rhetoric is bull! The question must be asked, why did President Bush choose these two blacks first? Was he trying to prove something? Of course he was and he didn't. He proved to black folks that he was just what we thought he was a pretender. In his mind he felt that if he choose these two token Negroes, he would prove that he had the Negroes interest and benefits in mind. Black folks don't just fall for anything. President Bush received approximately 6% of the African American vote during the presidential election.

We Know!

Black folks are well aware of the conspiracy of white folks. We may not say much, but we know. We know that we know because when we are not around white folks we talk about the "MAN" and the "SYSTEM" daily. We talk about how white folks treat us. We talk about how white folks view us. We talk about how white folks don't trust us. We talk about how many white folks feel that they are better than us.

We talk about how white folks don't want us living in their neighborhoods. We talk about how we train white folks on the job and they end up being our boss. We talk about how white folks stick up for one another.

We know and understand the white man's game. We don't say much but black folks are very well aware of how the system operates.

Many Republican, conservative politicians have said that there are no more free rides, referring to the blacks that are on welfare and those that receive government aid. It is ironic that the sons of slave owners who have been guilty of working slaves for four hundred years would so quickly come to the conclusion that they cannot help the very people that their fore-parents have been guilty of enslaving.

Now that we have entered in 2003 what will be the cry of the races? Shall we live together in a brotherhood? Will black folks and white folks realize that our entire destiny is tied up with one another!

Human-ship the tie that binds

My prayer for America and the world is that we will wake up and realize that within all of our bodies flow the red blood cells of life. Although our appearances are different and our skin comes in different shades we are still tied together in human-ship. That bond cannot and will not be severed. I pray that my white and black brothers will realize the urgency of the moment and move the barriers that have kept us separated from one another. Some theologians and philosophers have consistently preached and

taught that the world will remain just the way that it is because people will not change. I refuse to believe that people will not change. I believe that racism, prejudice and discrimination will be a thing of the past in the not to distance future. We must rise up above this stigma. I believe that the future will be promising. I believe that young whites and blacks that were born in the nineties and beyond will inherit a different kind of earth. I envision them inheriting an earth that is not sick and infested with the puss boils of racism. That is my prayer that is my hope.

Semi-Free

Are we really free? What is freedom? Black folks in America will never be free until we own machineries of mass production. We will not be free until we can control our own financial destinies. We will not be free until we can be self-sufficient. We will never be free until we can own our own, hire our own and pay our own. We will be free when we can own our own automobile factories, automobile car lots and financing corporations. We must become concentrate less on black power and concentrate more on green power. Black power without green power equals no power. Until we have our own and can be self-sufficient we are only semi-free.

Black folks feel that white folks here in America with the help of their ancestors perpetrated the greatest act of robbery and racketeering in the world upon the backs of slaves during slavery. And what really angers black folks is the fact that many white folks have the audacity to almost dare black folks to be mad or upset at white folks for slavery. Their arrogant attitudes seem to say to black folk hey, it happened now get over it.

Black folks will never forget that our ancestors were once slaves. White folks will never forget that their ancestors were once slave owners. As a result of these two scenarios black folks will always to some extent remain suspect to white folks. Many white folks feel that black folks have the same opportunities and chances for success as others and therefore should not be given preferential treatment.

It took white folks over 400 years to achieve the wealth that they have acquired here in America. How can they then expect black folks who are semi-free to gain equal footing in forty years?

Census Conspiracy

One of the greatest conspiracies in America involves the taking and counting of the census. White folks have purposely miscounted and not counted black folks in the census and for good reasons. White folks have repeatedly said that black folks only make up 12.7% of the population in America. White folks have also maintains that white folks make up approximately 73% of the population.

How can it be? Black folks were bred like animals for hundreds of years to populate plantations in the south. It was estimated that every state below the Mason-Dixon line had well over 50% black populations during the civil war. Black folks have continued to be fruitful and multiply since the civil war. White folks on the other hand have been very conservative when it has come to having children usually having one or two children. When we add up the math something seems to be out of sync. When black folks look at the census 73% Caucasian and 12.7% black it can seem discouraging to say the least. We know that power in America is acquired through the use of the ballot box. Whoever controls the ballot box will control America. If black folks can be fooled into believing that their vote will not count anyway and that they do not stand a chance of winning an election then we shall remain powerless. When white folks count the census they include (Germans, Irish, Jews, Italians, Hispanics, Asians, etc) as white while only African Americans are counted as blacks. America is usually broken up into two colors black and white. Black folks make up a greater segment of the population than what is represented in the census.

The bible says that everything that is done in the dark shall come to the light. We are entering into 2003 with open eyes and sharpened minds, inquisitive and proactive in every manner.

Black folks were not fooled during the presidential election of 2000. White folks proved to Americans black and white that they would be in power by any means necessary. They dismissed the votes of black folks and democrats in Florida and dared us to question their authority. That was a cold backhanded slap in the face to every black American citizen and democrat in the United States. And believe me black folks will never forget this! This was injustice to the tenth power!

I know that black folks in America for the most part are exploited and not given the same chances as white folks. We can live a lie but the truth will never die.

Educational Conspiracy

The conspiracy to retard black progress

Has it ever occurred to you that the only crime for which one is not eligible for Government student loans or government housing assistance is the conviction of drugs? Why is it so, you may ask? It's simple, because black folks are convicted of drug crimes at a rate of 5 to 1 when compared to whites.

A felony drug conviction is an automatically bar felons from student loans and many other government aids. This law has had a tremendous effect on reducing the number of African Americans entering into colleges and universities. Many black families are not able to afford college tuition. Now that black folks have realized that education is the key to better living, better jobs, better understanding of how the system operate, white folks have come up with all kinds of reasons, barriers, stumbling blocks and tests to prevent black folks from attaining a better education.

The Leap and Iowa tests began to surface in Louisiana during the early 1990's. In Louisiana the state instituted the Leap and Iowa test to evaluate student performance and to determine if students should be promoted to the next grade. These standardized tests backfired. Instead of hindering black children only many white children could not master these test. A loud cry was made by white folk and the tests were restructured. These tests proved to be unbeneficial to white folks in Louisiana. I personally believe that the intent of these tests is not to gauge performance but to create additional barriers and frustration. I said that this test would not last long in Louisiana because it was affecting to many white folks. In the last quarter of 2000, it was announced on television in Monroe, that the leap and Iowa test would be given but that it would not determine promotion or retention of students. The Praxis, GRE, LSAT and GMAT are additional examples of tests that are used to weed out black folks from certain programs. Education is and will continue to be the great equalizer.

Felons and the employment conspiracy

Why are so many black men in America unemployed? Felonies are a good place to start. Is it a coincidence that every job application asks the question, have you ever been convicted of a felony? African American males make up forty-eight percent of the prison population in America. Four out of every ten black men over the age of 30 have been convicted of a felony. White folks use felony convictions as barriers to justify not hiring African Americans.

Many ex-felons are barred from working on jobs that require;

a. One to carry a gun

b. A job that requires one to sell liquor

c. A job that requires you to work around money and children

When we step out of the box and look at the big picture ex-felons are not excluded from most jobs because they are not qualified, or lack the skills, but because they have been labeled for life.

This stigma of being an ex-felon is a never-ending story. Will the day ever come when I will no longer be required to list that I am an ex-felon on my application? I have paid my debt to society. Will my felony be forgiven in 10 years, 30, 40, 50, 100 years? Or am I destined to be attached to the body of this death forever? When!

When white folks use the ex-convict label against black folks they set us up for failure. When black folks are constantly denied employment and only given menial low-paying part-time jobs, they seek other alternatives to make money that will allow them to live out their dreams. These means may not be legal.

The Unjust Justice System

Before black folks allow their lawyers to talk them into a plea bargain for probation or a reduced felony they need to understand the consequences of a felony. When you are an ex-felon, you have a life sentence.

The juvenile justice and criminal justice system has done all but nail the last nail in the coffin for ex-felons. The juvenile justice and criminal justice system is a revolving door for ex-offenders. These systems are designed to return ex-felons to their cells. I personally believe that states are putting to much power into the hands of parole officers who can have an offender committed back into the department of corrections for any reason. Parole officers only have to believe that an offender is *about to commit a crime and that can serve as a basis for revocation.*

Revoking a person's probation or parole for merely thinking that they will commit a crime is clearly an abuse of discretion. When a person is sentenced to prison he is given a set number of years in the state of Louisiana. When he is placed into custody he is given a chance to opt for goodtime or he can elect to discharge on his fulltime discharge date. If he chooses to accept his goodtime date he is put to work and paid four cents an hour. This money is given back to the state in exchange for

42

his early release. This release takes place after the inmate has served 1/2 of his time.

Felons and Taxes: "No taxation without representation" What Happened?

The thirteen original colonies entered into a war with the British because they refused to pay taxes to England if they could not participate in electing the officials who would represent their interest.

What happened to these laws that the founding fathers enacted that forbid taxation without representation? Why are ex-felons in many American states forced to pay taxes yet they are not allowed to choose their representatives? What is the real purpose for not allowing ex-felons the right to vote? Is it really a way of teaching ex-felons a lesson, or is it a way of not letting ex-felons teach America a lesson?

Who will fight for the ex-felon's rights? I am confident that as we are propelled into the future we will witness the repealing, ratifying and decriminalization of many laws. I make this claim based on the premise that many celebrities, athletes and children from wealthy families will be arrested in the future and laws will be set in motion to reduce the get tough on crime stance.

I looked at the controversy that arose when Robert Downey Jr. was arrested in the later part of 2000. People began to ask the question did he do anything wrong? He was only hurting himself. He should not have to be locked up and caged like some animal. Who did he hurt? I concur with what they are saying, but I believe that they should have uttered that cry a long, long time ago.

Their are millions of black folks and poor folks that have been arrested and are currently doing time now because of the same crime that Robert Downey Jr. is charged with. As we reflect upon the indictments that were levied upon the president Bill Clinton, the arrest of prominent people like Sean Puffy Combs, Jason Williams, R. Kelly, Mystical, Governor Jab Bush's daughter, Robert Blake, Jim Brown, O.J., Governor Edwards in Louisiana, the insurance commissioner Jim Brown in Louisiana, Pee Wee Herman and many more we can expect nothing but change.

Most black folks believe that we have to many laws. If we continue to enact laws at the rate that we are going we will have to walk around with a criminal code just to make sure that our decisions and actions are not criminal. We have to many laws and every year the legislature convenes they are consistently adding more and more laws to the overcrowded criminal codes. This is ridiculous.

He that is without sin cast the first stone
America is full of criminals. Just because people are not arrested and prosecuted does not mean that they are not criminals. Many of America's best criminals will never be

arrested or prosecuted. I believe that Jesus made this statement to illustrate that no one is without fault and neither are we.

Many of us commit acts that can be defined as criminal on a daily basis and don't know it. My mother has always said that trouble is easy to get into but hard to get out. Momma is right! I have realized that she is so right. Yet, many folks white and black will never suffer prosecution because they know all of the right people and socialize with the right groups. Black folks believe that white folks always get off the hook or they receive less punishment than black folks in the courts. Black folks attribute this to the system. We have come accept this as being the American way.

Future Hope For Ex-Felons

I personally would like to see laws passed that will:

1. Allow felons the right to possess any license that he or she is otherwise qualified to hold, including but not limited to a license to practice law, M.D. licenses, any state, federal or city issued licenses. It is ridiculous that a felon cannot or is not supposed to hold a real estate license, what sense does that make? If a man get out of prison and has paid his debt to society and is trying to make a decent living for himself and his family why can't he or she be given a chance?

Are we inadvertently sentencing people to a life of hell without knowing it, or are we purposely allowing these Jim

Crow Laws, slave codes, black codes and ex-con codes to exist because we know that the majority of people affected by these laws are black and poor.

I am convinced that if the shoe was on the other foot and there was disproportionate majority confinement Americans would have declared imprisonment a national emergency.

2. Secondly, I would like to see a law passed that would allow ex-offender the right to live where they want, have a right to receive aid from the Government to pursue their educational goals. Black folks know that the juvenile justice and criminal justice system is not fair to minorities. We don't need research to prove this. Our proof is in our everyday experiences and encounters with system.

White folks know in their hearts that the system is unfair to blacks. Whites do not like to admit to this fact. Racism is alive and well in America.

3. Thirdly, I believe that an ex-felon should be allowed to hold political office. If voter have confidence in a person and they feel that this person can get the job done, they should be allowed to elect that person. Once again this law of not being able to hold public office or having to wait fifteen years after you are off of parole or probation to run for office is aimed at the ex-felon. These laws serve a two-fold purpose. As long as politicians are able to keep ex-felons out of the lawmaking process, they

will be able to keep the laws the way that they want them.

Certain laws have been enacted to target a certain population. Three strikes laws for instance are aimed primarily at black folks who are repeat offenders and these laws are used against black folks more often than any other race in America.

The get tough on drugs policy is really a get tough on black male drug dealer's drug policy. This get-tough approach has resulted in massive increases in the prison population for African American males and women. Crack cocaine arrests have caused the prison system to bulge at its' seam.

White folks who use cocaine as their drug of choice are exposed to less time for smoking pure cocaine than the black man is for smoking a derivative of cocaine. This is because black folks and the poor are the primary users of crack

4. Fourth, I would like to see a law passed that would make it illegal to require an ex-felon to divulge his criminal background to an employer unless it was a certain offense that had particular bearing on the job for which he/she was applying. Offenders should not be required to list their criminal convictions on application after five years have elapsed from their last discharge date. I know that there are certain offenses that may require

disclosure. Jobs that involve working with children or the infirm may require disclosure.

5. Ex-offenders should not be required to report to parole officers on a monthly basis, neither should they be required to pay a monthly fee in exchange for their freedom. The cost of operating the department of corrections should not be a burden to the offender, but should in effect be an expense of the Department of public safety and corrections. It is a shame that a man must spend years locked away from his family and then have to pay restitution and fees to remain free. Offenders did not create the department of corrections and should not have to work to keep it in operation.

If the Department of Corrections need additional money and cannot maintain their staff they need to reduce the amount of personnel that they have and not increase the burden of the offender. Offenders catch enough hell just trying to survive and keep their feet on solid ground. Black folk all over America know that the prison system is a warehouse for black men and that is what it is designed to be.

Black Man, Where art thou?

I shall never forget the awful sight of walking into a prison in Louisiana in 2000, looking at the black folks. When I walked into the prison dormitory there were black folks everywhere. A warehouse full of black folks all of them sitting on bunk beds. These black folks were triple bunked and had their under-wears, towels, socks and t-shirts hanging on the rails of the bunk beds.

I listened to the warden as he spoke of how the prison population would quadruple after the prison construction was complete. They were in a massive construction phase and to top it off they were using inmate carpenters, bricklayers, plumbers, sandblasters etc. The prisoners were building prisons for themselves, ironic as that may sound. I will be happy when prisoners wake up and allow the Department of Corrections to build their own prisons. I heard a black state legislator say that we know who the prisons are being built for and he was telling the true, these prisons were being and is being built for black men and women.

People who have completed their time in prison should be free to relocate to any place that they choose. There should be no restrictions placed on an offender in regards to his/her residence.

6. Ex-convicts should enjoy the right to consort with any person that they choose to consort with whether that person is a convict or not. Offenders should not have to worry about whether or not they are talking to an ex-felon. This scheme only serves as a mechanism to keep brothers who have gone through the system divided.

8. Any person that was not sentenced to pay restitution should not be compelled to pay restitution as part of the bargain to receive a pardon, commutation or suspension of sentence.

9. Finally a law should be passed to protect ex-felons who are violated while serving time on probation or parole. The person should be entitled to credit for time served while they were out in society. This is only right and just. Some people are released on 10 years of probation/parole and during their 9th year they are violated. They are then required to back-up the whole 10 years in prison. That to me is not fair. Credit should be given for the time that these felons have served successfully on the street.

The legislature's conspiracy to define criminal acts to hurt black folks

Why are offenders who are guilty of using pure cocaine exposed to a much less lighter sentence than those who use the derivative crack? Is it because black folks are arrested and convicted at a much higher rate for crack and white folks are arrested for the cocaine? The legislature is not interested in criminalizing the drug itself, but is merely interested in punishing black folks and using them to fill the jails and prisons so that business will continue as usual.

The laws of the United States are very ambiguous. These laws allow the wealthy to escape prosecution. The penalty for manslaughter used to be 20 years, but because white folks have allowed guns to infiltrate black folks neighborhoods and black folks have used guns on each other they have increased the sentence of manslaughter to 40 years. Who really benefits from this? Wall street investors and prison investors profit by the billions on longer sentences for blacks. The losers are the wives and children of those locked up. The black communities are the losers.

Unwarranted Fear

Black folks know that white folks fear what might happen if black folks ever acquire political and economic leverage. According to the census predictions by the year 2016 if not sooner white folk will fall into the minority class and Hispanics will constitute the majority. That's another big lie! How in the hell can Hispanics make up the majority when black folks out number them 3 to 1 right now in America? Black people are still having babies and will continue to have them.

If I was President of the United States

If I am ever elected President of the United States my first executive order would be to release all drug users and petty criminals who are no threat to society.

I would pardon crack addicts and petty criminals in a heartbeat. This directive would result in the removal of 80% of the prison population. Black folks are well aware of the fact that prisonization is a business in America. Black folks are not fooled into believing that prisons are only used to keep the streets in America safe.

Eugenics (Population control)

The incarceration of hundreds of thousands of black folks is the greatest act of eugenics that the world has ever seen. If black folks are locked up they cannot reproduce. Black folks are disproportion ally confined in America and South Africa. White folks cannot continue to lock black folks up and think that they can stop us. It will not work. Approximately 1.2 million black men are locked up in America today in 2003. Another 6 million blacks are disenfranchised (cannot vote) because white folks fear what will happen if these black folks wake up and realize the multitudes of power that we possess at the ballot box.

If black folks were released from jails and prisons we would have many more babies. White folks pay black folks not to have babies. They give them free birth control. They sterilize our women. Why? Because every warm body represent a vote. If black folks are released in large numbers we will witness an explosion in our population growth.

If white folks can continue to keep black men locked up in prison he knows that the black population will suffer. This is planned out eugenics.

If the white man can maintain large numbers in the population he knows that he can stay in power. Voting is the key to power.

When blacks finally wake up and vote chances are that white folks will change the rules of the game. White folks have proved to America what they can and will do if their political or economic power is threatened.

White folks have every right to be fearful of black folks in this respect. Hubert Blalock's Power Threat Theory of 1967 alluded to the fact that anytime their was an increase in minority concentration the majority would resort to any means necessary to make sure that they stayed in power. White folks in 2003 are still doing the same thing. Power is never given up freely.

The two-faces of justice

While attending graduate school at the University of Louisiana at Monroe one of my professors stated to the class that she had a friend who was guilty of DWI and vehicular homicide. That family contacted a lawyer who knew the D.A. in that parish. The lawyer requested a fee of ten thousand dollars and the accused and his case never made it to the docket. Welcome to White Justice in America! To say that blacks only make up 12.7 % of the population, (which is an outright lie), isn't it strange and baffling that blacks make up approximately 50% of the prison population?

When white folks are arrested many of them are referred to treatment and rehabilitation programs. White folks are given numerous chances to make amends before they are committed to jails or prisons.

53

What White Folks and the Media Don't report about Black Folks

Being black in a White dominated society is challenging to say the least. Black folks must always remember who we are and whom we are dealing with. Most black folks including myself know that there are many white folks who do not care for us. White folks tolerate black folks because they know that they are responsible for the present conditions of black folks in America. I find it rather strange that many white folks will harp on the fact that education is free and anyone can go to college. White folks say that black people are in the shape that they are in because they choose not to take advantage of the programs that are offered to them. White folks will say that quick, fast and in a hurry. What I don't hear white folks say is that slavery has handicapped the entire black race. I do not hear white folks say that black folks must play catch up and that they have a 400year head start. I do not hear white folks say that black folks have progressed well considering the fact that less than fifty years ago,

a. They could not vote freely,
b. Could not ride in the front of the bus,
c. Lived in segregated housing
d. Were denied many jobs because of the color of their skin
e. Subjected to inadequate education

54

f.   Treated unfairly in the courts (this is still true today)

It was only 35 years ago that James Earl Ray who some say was hired by the FBI assassinated Dr. Martin Luther King in Memphis Tennessee.

I am personally proud of the accomplishments that black folks have made in this short period of time. Black folks have improved in many areas including education, politics, religion, wealth, business ownership, and increasing personal assets.

Today, we have more black Governors, Mayors, Legislators, Senators, City Councilmen, Police Chiefs, Business Owners, Home Owners, CEO's of Fortune Five Hundred Companies, High School and College Graduates, Millionaire Athletes and Entertainers etc. Black folks are on the move in America and will continue to make strides with the help of God.

The media does not report many positive accomplishments of blacks in America. Most of the news that black folks hear from the media is negative news. Black folks are entering and graduating from college in large numbers but we don't here that from the media. Black folks are starting businesses and buying homes. Black folks are sending their children to colleges and universities in record numbers but we don't hear that. We have a long way to go but I am confident that we will reach our goal.

White folks are not quick to report news that put black Americans in the positive spotlight. That is why we need black own radio and television stations and anchors like Tavis Smiley. We also need radio talk show hosts like Tom Joyner.

The Prison Conspiracy

What is the real purpose of the prison system? To what extent are prisons (moneymaking industrial complexes) designed by rich white folks and profitable for companies on Wall Street? Who is putting up these billions of dollars to build all of these prisons? Insurance companies and private investors put up billions of dollars each year to continue their business as usual projects.

Every year billions of dollars are spent on building prisons and caring for prisoners. The prison population never decreases. Have we stopped to think about the true role that prisons plays in our society? Some folk think that prison is designed to lock up bad people and keep them off the streets. We need to think again!

Prison, Money, and Politics

Black folks know that we need prisons in America. We must not forget that prisons are also moneymaking organizations also. White folks are getting wealthy from the exploitation of black folks in the prison system. The prison industry drains the federal government of approximately 640 billion dollars each year. It is a shame and a travesty of justice that white folks will exploit black folks and value dollar bills over black families staying intact.

Over seventy percent of the people in prison do not have to be there. Black folks know that but these folks are there because of dollars not sense. Only ten to fifteen percent of the people in prison are there because of some violent act that they have committed. Large insurance companies invest money in the prison industrial complex to build prisons. The federal government guarantees these corporations very high returns.

Do we really need to continue to build prisons every year? Is it possible for offenders to benefit from drug rehab programs and community services programs? Of course, but what will happen to the dividends of the wealthy stock companies and the steel and concrete industries?

Black Prison Population

Today in America there are approximately 1.2 million black men in their child producing ages locked up behind bars. Incarceration has reduced the birth rates of African Americans by 500,000 to 1.5 million per year. I believe that white folks will do anything necessary to stop black people from gaining equal power with them even if it means incarcerating the whole African American race. I also believe that if it becomes necessary President Bush will drop a nuclear bomb on Iraq or North Korea to maintain the status quo of Americans.

When black men are incarcerated white men usually assume power over the black family especially if the family has to depend on the system for support.

The real deal on why black folks are locked up

Prison is a big business for white folks. Black folks are being warehoused and exploited because white folks need jobs to pay their bills. White folks don't care about locking up black folks. We should have figured this out long time ago. That should have been evident when we realized that they have different penalties for folks who smoke crack cocaine and those who snort powder cocaine.

What's good for the goose should be good for the gander. I firmly believe that if the powder cocaine was the drug of choice for black folks and crack was the drug of choice for white folks the sentences would be reversed. One politician made the statement that he was not concerned about the people being arrested for crack because they were not his constituents. That is just like saying I don't care what kind of sentence they get either.

I have constantly asked myself what is it about the black man that the white man fear so much? Why does he fear a black government? Why does he preach against the commingling of the races? Why do he preach and teach holy Christian love and unity in church and practice separation and partiality in society?

The exploitation of prisoners is such a great injustice. It is a shame that white folks who are our lawmakers separate little children from their mothers and fathers because they have created environments in which people try to escape their misery through the use of drugs. Women young and old sell their bodies to make ends meet. Men young and old sell drugs to get the things that they want and need. Many become addicted to drugs and alcohol because of the pressures of life. These black folks get desperate because they are tired of struggling and being broke and they commit crimes.

Is it the prisoner's fault because he committed a crime? Or is it societies fault that the prisoner committed a crime because he was not provided a decent job. Capitalism is the cause of many ills in America including the swelling of the prison system. Today white folks have turned the prison system into a multi-billion dollar business.

Why white folks don't want black folks out of Prison

Don't think for one minute that it has not occurred to black people that the reason that so many blacks are incarcerated is to slow down the populating of blacks in America. Its called eugenics or population control. The white man knows that blacks love to have sex including myself. The white man also knows that when people have unprotected sex babies are born. We must never cease to remember that every black baby born represents a vote. Just think with the right kind of population blacks can rule and run America. But black folks are not interested in running America we are only concerned about being treated fairly.

Population is power, but population with voting power is ultimate power. That is why 14 states in the U.S. strip ex-felons of their voting rights. Votes represent power and the white man want you to be powerless that is why he enact laws to convict you of felonies and then he keep you away from the ballot box by saying you committed a crime so your citizenship rights are revoked. Wake up!

White folks will do anything and go to any extremes to make sure that black folks do not outnumber them at the polls. The polls are dangerous and the white man knows that. Not if, but When the black man wake up and realize how much power he really have when he vote as a bloc, the world as we know it will never be the same. Black folks will start enjoying the fruits of their labor and the labor of our forefathers. I believe that black folks will be honest and upright with white folks when the day comes because we know how it feel to be exploited and mistreated. I believe along with Dr. King that Black Supremacy is as dangerous as White Supremacy.

What every black person in prison should do NOW!

If black folks wanted to reduce the prison population all they have to do is one thing. STOP WORKING! If inmates ever wake up, I don't care if they are locked up in the city, Parish,

County, state or federal jails or penitentiary, and just stop working and say take me to lockdown the prison system would shut down. If inmates begin to tell correctional officers that they don't want to work no more and that they are willing to do their time flat.

The Future Bankruptcy Of The Prison System In America (2003-2006)

The prison system cannot continue to operate at its business as usual capacity. The prison system is spending too much money on inmates and too little on education, Medicare, Medicaid, social services programs and elderly prescription to name a few things. The media and politicians have citizens hyped up believing that criminals are so dangerous. That is bull. Only approximately 10-15 percent of prisoners are in prison for serious violent crimes. Most people in prisons and jails are there for property crimes and drug offenses. When most white folks hear the word crime they automatically picture black folks. Therefore they become more punitive and retributive when it comes to punishment. I also believe that criminals should be locked up. But I also believe that the punishment should fit the crime. It does not make sense to lock up all of these dope feigns and crack heads and not get them any help. Drug addiction is an illness and requires treatment. We cannot rehabilitate an addict by throwing him or her in a prison cell and slamming the door shut. These people need treatment. That is why I would not be

61

mad at inmates if they just stopped working and shut the system down. The prison system cannot survive without the aid of the inmates.

It is wrong to give all of these black folks thirty, forty and fifty years in prison for possession with intent to distribute. I know that folks must be held accountable for their actions but that works both ways. Society must be held responsible for the subtle acts of racism and prejudices that exist in employment sectors in America.

We can reduce crime significantly if we give black folks jobs. Black folks want to work but we will not work for nothing. Many folks are quick to say that black folks should take any jobs that they can get and try to improve their skills and change jobs. I do agree with the fact that we should take advantage of all opportunities but I also know that it is not as easy as black and white folks think it is to get a job at McDonalds or other minimum paying jobs. If Americans are serious about reducing crimes they will provide jobs for all people in society. We are not laying down and accepting the fact that white folks get all of the good paying, supervisory, management jobs and the black folks get what is left. That is not right.

If black folks made the amounts of money that white folks made they to would stay home and smoke and snort their drugs in their suburban homes. They would find other activities and hobbies such as golf, hunting and fishing.

Cornell West's book race matter is a very good book. Race does matter in everything that we do in my opinion. I also believe that money matters also. Middle-class and wealthy people don't go to jail or prison. They have enough money to get anything that they want and can also hire them a lawyer if they should get caught. Poor folks don't have that luxury! Black folks must wake up in the prison systems.

If inmates peacefully stop working the prisons and jails will be forced to hire people to cook, clean-up, wash clothes, buff and shine floors, cut the grass outside, tend to the fields, gardens, livestock, build desks, print stationary, hire real lawyers off the street, hire real construction crews to build prisons and other buildings. If this is done on a widespread scale the prison systems as we know it would certainly go bankrupt.

It is important that we understand and realize that prisoners are the ones that keep the prison system operating in full capacity.

Without the labor of the prisoners, the prison system could not survive; the prison system is a parasite that dependents on the labor and skills of those who are imprisoned. The prison system is a leech that attaches itself to the leg of the inmate and cannot survive very long without his blood. If inmates don't cook, cleanup, wash, build, drill, buy, cry, hide, lie, cut grass, fight, curse, or sway. Help will be on the way.

Common Sense!

Why does America continue to spend 20-30 thousand dollars a year to incarcerate a crack addict and will not spend 15,000 to employ a crack addict on the street? If America employed black folks and poor folks they would not be so stressed, depressed and hopeless and maybe they could become law-abiding, tax-paying citizens. It is a shame that teachers are being laid off, students have larger classrooms, social service programs are being cut at astronomical rates, elderly people are having to pay more for health care and prescriptions, city and state employees are being laid off because of budget shortfalls. Everyone is losing and it is all because the U.S. believes that they can solve the crime problem by locking us the poor and the underclass. Confinement is not the answer to the woes of America. Employment is the answer. It is such a shame and disgrace that the prison systems have 0% unemployment and they can find every man in prison a job but cannot help them when they are released.

Most prison wardens will tell you that inmates must work so that they can stay occupied because that reduces their stress and their chances of getting in trouble on the compound. Those statements are golden. I only hope that they would tell this to the President of the U.S. If work reduces crime in prison it would do the same thing in the free world.

Creation Of Unjust Laws In America

Job Security At The Expense Of Black Folks.

The United States and South Africa lead the world in incarceration rates. The United States and South Africa are

64

similar in that they both practiced dehumanization methods. The United States enslaved millions of blacks through slavery and the people of South Africa enslaved millions of South Africans through apartheid, today both of these countries have the largest number of prisoners in the world per capita.

Plantation owners whipped slaves who broke the law prior to 1863. Slaves were the exclusive property of the plantation owners. Black folks were not sent to prison prior to the Civil War. After the emancipation proclamation in 1863, the bill of rights guaranteed the slaves equal protection under the law in the first, eighth and fifth amendments.

Before slaves were set free they had no problems with obeying the law when prisons became very popular in the late 1800's and the early 1900's the theme and conspiracy was to incarcerate the newly freed slaves. It was during this time that the convict lease system became popular. The convict lease system was used as a mechanism to return the freed slaves back to the plantation owners.

The convict lease system allowed those arrested slaves to be leased to private companies. These companies had complete charge over these freed slaves. These slaves were worked hard building bridges and railroads. They were used to cultivate fields and pick cotton. These prisoners were not dangerous men. These men were arrested for vagrancy. They were arrested for not being able to pay their poll taxes. They were arrested for not have a permanent place of residence.

These prison institutions were receiving local, state and federal monies to house inmates and feed them. These companies were making money through both spectrums. They made money from the private companies that leased the prisoners and from the governmental entities that supported the prisons.

Prison officials and administrators recognized the profitability of incarceration after private companies pumped millions into the states economy through the use of the convict lease system. Best of all the convict lease system was protected by the United States constitution.

White folks in America today are still profiting off of the exploitation of black folks. There is only one way in which slavery is still permitted in the United States in 2003. Slavery is permitted only in prison institutions. Check your state constitution. Many folks believe that slavery is illegal but it is not. Slavery is still legal in the prison system. White folks in America enslave millions of people and make a hell of a profit while doing it. They do all of this under the auspice of protecting the American people.

Protecting the American people from super predators

American politicians and news media are famous for scaring the public into believing that there are vicious killers and rapists in their communities. They are gifted in having people panic and believe that the streets are unsafe.

Who are they protecting? When I say they I am referring to the white lawmakers, policy makers and governmental officials who are responsible for enacting laws that affect the prison system and our communities. Are these politicians really concerned about the safety of America? America's safety in many instances is the farthest thing from the minds of politicians. The streets are not safer today in 2003 than they were in 1963. Incarceration has skyrocketed and black folks have continued to be the scapegoat for American warehousing. We can spend billions of dollars and lock up every Tom, Dick, Harry, Willie and Bubba, but that in it self will not cure the crime problem.

The Voting Conspiracy

Florida taught black folks all over America a lesson that money cannot buy! Florida show black folks that white folks have been pulling the wool over our eyes for a long time. Our votes have been getting lost in the shuffle for a long time. First white folks did not want black folks to vote. The Klu Klux Klan did their best to scare black folks through lynching. Now that we have gained the right to vote white folks will not count our vote correctly.

White folks have lied to black folks for a long time. White folks have fooled black folks with the census. They tell us that we do not have the numbers to win many elections. Black folks are waking up in America today and realizing that it is not the numbers that we don't have, it is the right methods of counting the votes that are missing. Those who have perpetrated this scheme are very aware of what they are doing. We must realize that voting machines are man-made and therefore are subject to manipulation by man.

Black folks all over America believe that a new method should be adopted for counting votes. Black folks have been cheated, robbed and exploited long enough at the voting booth. During the last presidential election black folks had the oldest and most outdated machines in their voting precincts. Many of these machines had an accurate ratio of 7 to 1.

Bloc-Voting Power

White folks tell us that our numbers don't add up and that we cannot elect a black mayor, governor or president because we just don't have the numbers. Don't be fool! The people in the Census Bureau lie just like anybody else. Mayor Lee P. Brown of Houston was elect to several terms as mayor of Houston despite the census saying that Houston is comprised of only 26% blacks.

The Klan Strain

The American Klan terrorized black folks who spoke out for their rights to vote. When Malcolm X's father the Rev. Earl Little spoke up for the Marcus Garvey movement he was run over by a train at the hands of the Klan in Lansing Michigan. The Klan because of his stance for equal rights, which included the right to vote, gunned down Medgar Evers. Four beautiful young black children were killed at Dexter Ave Baptist Church in Birmingham, Alabama by racist whites that did not want to see blacks achieve equality and the list goes on and on. When we speak of the Klan, we must understand that the Klan consisted of policeman, lawyers, judges, sheriffs, preachers etc. A white Southern Baptist Preacher in Georgia started the Klan. The Klan of 2003 consists of the same types of people. Today you can find the Klan in many places. The Klan is represented on many police forces, in the District Attorney's Office, CEO'S of Banks, Teachers, Professors, Managers of fast food Restaurants, City Workers, Pastors of Large churches of all denominations etc. The Klan still has the same objective after all of these years and that objective has been and still is to keep black folks Powerless in America.

Cleo Fields made a very surprising remark during his campaign for senator in Baton Rouge Parish in 1995. Senator Fields commented on the fact that the lines in his district were being redrawn to dilute the voting power of African Americans. The lines were being drawn in such a manner that a strong white opponent would be able to easily win a seat in his district. Some of us have referred to this practice of changing the racial make up of a district to benefit a certain group as gerrymandering. When we see new housing projects being built in sparsely populated suburban area, what we are really seeing is gerrymandering. Actions such as these are strategically designed to keep the powers that be in power. When we analyze the facts we quickly realize that this whole system is designed to keep white folks in power and keep the black folks divided.

White Neighbor Black Neighbor

Most white folks do not want black neighbors. Lets be real. White folks who can afford to leave areas that are infiltrated with blacks will quickly and gladly leave. They say that black folks do not keep their property up and they say that when blacks move into the neighborhood the their property values are reduced. This is not a myth. Banks and lending institutions will decrease the value of property when blacks move into the hood. We know that white folks do not want to live around black folks. Politicians know this also. So why would white politicians who have the power to build projects in any area of a city choose to place projects that will be filled with blacks in suburban communities? When these new projects were being built in the suburbs it was not to integrate the neighborhoods and they were not being built to increase the tax base of the community. These projects were being built and strategically placed in these suburban neighborhoods to dilute the black vote. City administrators very carefully plan these decisions. These administrators know exactly what they are doing. These housing projects were not placed in the heart of Dixie. They were not in the prime communities of white people. They were put in areas that were sparsely populated. White administrators would find

70

parcels of land in certain areas and throw up a project to keep black folks divided and unable to bloc-vote.

The Welfare Conspiracy

The welfare conspiracy is the best-kept secret in America. White folks have stayed in power by encouraging black folks to remain perpetually dependent through the welfare system. Welfare was intended to temporarily help people who needed assistance until they could regain their footing. Welfare has caused generation after generation of black folks to rely on meager substances barely making it, while white folks ran your life. The white man becomes Jesus and the 1st thru 7th is mother's day for welfare recipients. It is very apparent that welfare is needed but the United States government can provide jobs to help poor people so that they would not have to be on welfare for the rest of their lives.

The government spends billions of dollars to pay for housing, Medicare, AFDC, WIC, utility stipends, food stamps etc? If the government can afford to spend billions of dollars to keep folks on welfare wouldn't it seem wise for the government to develop jobs to make these folks independent and productive citizens?

Many people may ask themselves is welfare a means to an end or an end to a means. Welfare is a system that has been set up in America to do just what it is doing. One thing that has bothered me personally about the welfare system is the way in which those who receive aid are viewed. The recipients of welfare are

71

viewed as being lazy, uneducated, content, and in some cases happy with their present condition. How can that be? People who are on the outside looking in don't really get the whole picture. Why would someone be happy receiving 214.00 per month and having to use it to make ends meet for themselves and their 3 children. These meager government assistances are used to purchase food, pay the subsidized rent, and pay utilities. The rest of their government aid is in the form of food stamps that can only be used to buy food.

Foolish Spending

Americans will spend billions of dollars cloning animals, building missile defense systems, exploring space, fighting wars etc. When is comes to providing government aid to families in need and providing assistance to the homeless, and the elderly American politicians cry foul. It does not take a rocket scientist to figure out that Americans have their priorities in the wrong place. This country can eradicate homelessness and poverty. We have the resources to reduce crime and put all Americans to work.

The government will spend billions of dollars on cloning an animal but refuse to make sure that every kid in America is immunized and have adequate shelter. The government will not spend money to make sure that each kid receive a competent education and live in a safe environment, yet we spend billions of dollars sending men to the moon. Humans will never live on the moon or mars. There are some things that we can do without.   Welfare should not be a problem. Welfare should be part of a solution.

Welfare should be available as a safety net for those that need help. We make a big deal about people being on welfare and not wanting to work. We should be trying to evaluate their reasons for not wanting to leave the comfort zones. Many of these people leave welfare to work for menial jobs that pay minimum wage. Welfare is part of the structure of American society. Welfare is perpetrated on the masses of people to keep them in a position of dependence.

If the United States government spent the same amount of money on residents that they spent giving to the housing projects, WIC, AFDC, food stamps, Medicare etc things would be much better. If jobs were created for people on welfare and they were allowed to earn money and given a chance to buy their apartments and houses things would be much better.

Christ Conspiracy

THE CONSPIRACY TO CREATE A CHRIST: MY VIEWS ON RELIGION THEN AND NOW!

All of my life, I have grown up hearing older people say don't question God. I have read passages in the bible that has said avoid foolish questions and genealogies, which stir up strife. I have read passages in the book of Romans that says slaves obey your masters, for this is right in the eyes of the Lord, not with just eye service as men pleasers but with work and in this passage God is quoted as saying that he is no respecter of persons. I have read extensively about people who lived during the same era as it is reported that Christ lived and in all of their memoirs, none of them have reported any strange or unusual happenings or healings etc.

I have read about Sir David Livingston, the white European Missionary that went into Africa with his bible in his hand preaching about Jesus and salvation to Africans. Livingston it is reported acquired vast amounts of riches from Africans including land, natural resources, diamonds and other precious jewels. David Livingston went into Africa with just his bible in his hand and when he left Africa it is reported that the Africans had the bible and he had all of their deeds to their land.

We dare not stop there. The great psychologist Sigmund Freud who considered himself an atheist said in retrospect that Religion was a great farce that was designed to allow poor people to have hope for the future and something positive that they could look forward to after their lives of misery on earth. It was believed by Freud that if the masses of poor people woke-up out of their trance and realized that they were dammed to die a hopeless, miserable life on earth, they would be more susceptible to creating uprisings.

In this respect religion is a mechanism used to keep the masses of poor people quiet and to take their minds off of their positions and places in society. In the western hemisphere their is no doubt that the people who are most closely associated to the church and have the greatest belief in God are normally poor people or people who grew up poor.

The church of today in an effort to console and comfort parishioners have constantly reminded them of their hope beyond this life. Heaven is always looked upon as a jubilant place. Heaven is viewed as a place where people can lay their burdens down. To be Christian means that one must assume that it is acceptable to be burdened as we live in this life.

When black folks die the preacher always tell the audience that we are here for a home going celebration. We know that everyone that dies will not go to heaven. Some funerals are not celebrations but disasters. Yet, we comfort the bereaved families in the same manner, even if we had prior knowledge of the deceased sinful life. I am not trying to judge any man. I am only trying to make a point. I realize that people change and that they may have death bed conversions.

Hope Mechanism

This is the hope mechanism. In the black community when folks die we constantly say and believe that this person is going to a better place. We say this to comfort one another but in reality we don't know what happens to the dead. We don't have any friends that have died and came back after two or three years to tell us what happens to the dead when they die.

Are we really fooling ourselves? Do we really believe in God? Do we really believe that our love ones is going to a better place? If we really believed that they were going to a better place why are we so sad at funerals? Why are we so distraught at learning of their demise?

Is the church a hope mechanism for the poor, oppressed, exploited, hopeless masses of people in the world! There are so many different cultures, gods, and beliefs that exist in our world today. According to western civilization God is supreme and if man does not accept Jesus Christ as their personal savior they are destined to be hell bound.

Paul goes on to say that if anyone comes with any other doctrine not only do you not accept them but don't even bid them Godspeed. Well we know for a fact that there are billions of people in the world that do not believe in the God that we believe in. Are all of these people automatically going to hell? Yes, according to the Christian bible.

When I think about the teachings of the bible and the beliefs of the people who study and live Christian lives it is easy to establish disturbing paradoxes. Are we worshiping God because we love God or are we worshiping God to avoid the consequences of going to hell?

When we view Christianity in this respect it seems that God is saying to us that if we don't worship him he will reward us with eternal damnation. In this respect religion is coerced on the people and not a matter of free will.

"Slaves obey your masters"

One other thing that has caused much attention to be given to the authenticity of religion is the fact that slave masters used religion as a mechanism to keep slaves in line. Religion offered slaves a new better life in the heavens with God. How ironic! Slaves viewed this as if religion meant that God was good, but he could not offer them a good life on earth. These slaves felt that it was God's will for them to toil and sweat for master slave owner here on this earth, but when they would die and go up yonder they would be free and rejoicing, no more slave master.

How absurd! In the book *"Slave Community"*. The author illustrates that slave masters only allowed certain types of sermons to be preached to the slaves. Many slaves attended church either under a white preacher or a black preacher who were both instructed on what to preach. Slave owners or plantation overseers were always present during church services. They were there to monitor the messages that the preacher preached and to make sure that the slaves were not planning any uprisings.

One of the most favorite Sunday sermons for the overseers and slave masters was found in the book of Romans which said slaves obey your masters for this is pleasing in the eyes of the Lord. How clever! The sermons were preached to make the slave feel that he must work hard for the taskmaster. These sermons made the slaves believe that their hard work was pleasing to God and would earn them a later reward of eternal life.

Finally, I am concerned with the origin story of the bible. In the beginning God created Adam and Eve. They were the only two people on earth. Adam and Eve gave birth to Cain and Abel. According to the bible after Cain killed his brother Abel he was labeled a vagabond and wandered into another country. God said that no one should hurt Cain and that he had placed a mark on him. Cain met a lady that became his wife in that country. Where did she come from if Adam and Eve were the only people on the earth?

Did I miss something? or is this one of those questions that we are not supposed to ask? The story of the birth of Rome is rather fascinating to me because in this story we have the same story of the birth and death of Cain and Abel. The only noticeable difference is the names that are used Remus and Romulus. Everything else is quite the same. What becomes even more fascinating is the fact that the story of the birth of Rome was written thousand of years before the writings of the bible. Did the writers of the bible borrow certain stories from other cultures such as the Romans? Maybe!

My Beliefs

I do believe in God, but not to the extent that I cannot ask questions. I will not allow my self to be exploited through religion. I will not allow religion to serve as a sleeping pill for the masses. We must be willing to engage in peaceful protest.

We must not allow our religion to give us the comforts of a better tomorrow while allowing us to accept the hell that we catch in America today. We must not allow our Christian beliefs to prevent us from voicing our opinions and concerns.

"What Church Means To Me"

Church was not an option when I was growing up. My mother made it mandatory that we attended church. I have always attended church all of my life. The thing that I remember most about church when I was growing up was an incident that I do not talk about much because I've felt that people would not believe me.

I remember coming home from a revival when I was a young boy around ten years old. The preacher said that that night that God could do anything and that he was real. There was a broken clock on our kitchen table. This clock had a winding spring. I asked the lord to make that clock work if he was real. The next morning when I awoke, I went straight for the clock. I picked it up back still off and the clock was ticking. I will never forget that. Was this a coincidence? I don't know, but I do know that the clock was not ticking when I went to bed that night and it was ticking when I woke up.

We grew up in two different churches in Crowley Louisiana. We attended Israelite Baptist church where Rev. Grady Poullard was pastor and we attended First Church Of God In Christ where Elder Roy Winbush was pastor. Elder Winbush is now Bishop Roy Winbush.

Church was always exciting to me and we learned a lot about the bible and God. I was baptized at an early age in both churches. My brothers always went to church. We sung in the choir. Sometimes my mother would come with us to church. But she always made sure we went. We did not play in church. My mother could just look at us in church and we knew what that look meant. We would be still and quite. She did not make any promises that she did not keep. When she said she was going to whip you she did. Sometimes we would forget because of the time that had passed, but momma did not forget. When it was time for a whipping in my house we really begged and pleaded. You did not care if others teased you later you did some serious pleading to avoid a whipping in my house.

My brothers and I would start crying and hollering I am sorry momma. I am not going to do it no more. Yes right! Like that helped. Momma would get that extension cord and tell us it is going to hurt her more than it would hurt us. She would grab your hand with one hand and the extension cord went to work. It was like being on a merry go-round. She did not let you go until she was finish. I don't care how loud you hollered and fell on the floor momma resurrected you with that extension cord.

One day my brother Percy and I who my momma called Heckle and Jeckle because if you gave him something you had to give me the same thing decided to play our favorite game on momma. While momma was on the phone he and I use to play a game called how loud. We would see who could curse the loudest in a disguised voice while momma was on the telephone. We would curse, but we did it in a manner where she did not really understand exactly what we were saying. One-day momma got off the phone and told us to come with her and Lord she whipped us good. She did not spare any licks with that extension cord. That was the end of our cursing game for life. All of my brothers and sisters in my family believe in God. You may not be able to tell it based on the way we live sometimes, but we do believe in the Lord.

The Reason White Folk Hate Rap Music (Ghetto Newspapers)

Ghetto Newspapers

Rap music is nothing more than ghetto newspapers. There are many white folks and some misinformed black folks that rush to judge rap music as being demeaning, vulgar, disrespectful etc. How can something that is true be so bad? How can something that is so right be so wrong? Let me say first of all that I love Tupac, NWA, Ice Cube, Ice T, Snoop and the whole gangsta rap family. I love all music but especially rap and gospel. It is my prayer that gangsta rap never die. Keep making that Gangsta Rap. These young black brothers and sisters are just telling the world how it feels to be black, poor, disrespected, exploited, unemployed, misused and mad as hell in America. Gangsta rap is an outlet for inner city and suburban young blacks to express themselves. White folks have had the media outlets tied up for a very long time.

Black folks must never stop passing out ghetto newspapers. Keep rhyming and spitting gangsta rap. Until we are free keep busting lyrics, don't bite your tongue, tell the truth. Tell it like it is. If white folks or black folks don't like what you are saying, tell them to change the situations and if situations change the rap will change also.

The World That I See

The world that I see is a very different world than the one that I live in. I see a world where people can live in peace and harmony with one another. I see a world where all citizens will be provided with conventional means to meet their goals. I see a different world and different people. I see a world in which people will care about one another. These people will be willing to give more than they take. I envision a world in which resources will be pooled and set aside for future generations. I see a world in which the government will be more concerned with meeting the needs of the people. Technology and research exploration will not be valued over the needs of people. This nation will never rise above its lowest citizen.

We can save our youth by providing free computers and Internet services to every home in America. We can save our youth by offering them 2,500.00 for every student that graduate from school without children. We can save our youth by providing families with yearly allowances of 1500.00 per child. This money will help children explore and travel to other places in America. Children should be exposed to other cities and environments so that they will be know that there are other places that exist. I envision a world in which the church communities will become more active in the lives of children and adults. I envision a world where all children are properly immunized and given a decent education. No child will be left behind.

"Some Of My Best Friends Are Black "

I would guess that we all can count on our fingers and toes the amount of times that we have met white folks who have mentioned that one of their best friends are black. Hooray! But what is that suppose to mean? Because one of your friends is black, does that mean that you love black people? Do that mean that you are willing to accept other black people that fit the criteria and descriptions of your friend or is that a fancy way of saying that you are not prejudice or racist to any great degree? In my opinion people who are quick to say this have already blown their cover with me. When statements of this nature are made it gives you the impression that this person is very conscious of race.

I cannot see myself meeting with other white folks and telling them that some of my best friends are white. So What! I have had very many experiences with white people, some of the experiences were good and some were bad, but the thing that sticks out the most involving my relationship with white folks is the set manner in which they expect you to act or perform. Very many white folks expect black folks to stay in their place. If you cross the line white folks view you as a suspect, a troublemaker or an agitator. I have always been a free black man. I was born free and there is no doubt in my mind that I will die free! I have spoken my mind in the past and I am planning on speaking my mind in the future.

Future pay checks

White folks are still locking up black folks in astronomical numbers and throwing away the key because black folks are continuing to get addicted to drugs that white folks are constantly putting in black neighborhoods. Black folks do not fly to the jungles of South America and pick up cocaine to make crack. Black folks do not navigate ships to South America to pick up tons of coca powder to bring back to the lab.

White folks have had the dope game on lock from the jump and they continue to make billions of dollars on black folks through the drug trade. White folks win in both ways. When black folks buy drugs white folks get paid because they are suppliers and when black folks go to jail white folks get paid because they are

Judges, District Attorneys, Policemen, Correctional Officers etc. The sad part of this story is that the U.S. government can reduce the flow of drugs that is piped into the U.S.

What Black Folks In America Should Do Now

I watched the state of the black church, which was recorded in Detroit with Tavis and Tom. Mayor Kilpatrick it did my heart well to see a young black brother running the city. Earring in ear and as articulate as they come. Congratulation Mayor Kilpatrick. The church has millions of dollars in wealth. We can come together! We can build our own communities and open our own businesses.

I am not a separatist, but it comes a time in life when you tired of begging, pleading and knocking at the door and you know that white folks hear you but they will not let you in. Therefore you dry your tears and build your own.

Come together! I would love to see every black church in every city in America come together. We must pool our monies together and open up businesses. We can begin with businesses such as grocery stores, food restaurants, clothing stores, car dealerships, residential and commercial construction companies, banks and credit unions etc. If we are to ever reach our plateau in this life these things must come to pass. If we take inventory, we already have what we need to get started. Black folks spend approximately three hundred billion dollars per year.

Black churches have credit and borrowing power. We have CPA's and expendable monies. If black folks pulled their resources together our accomplishments would be much and mighty. We would be in position to control our own destiny! We would no longer be compelled to sit and beg praying for acceptance from white folks and white institutions if we had our own. Money offers a certain degree of security and acceptance to its bearer. We can chart our own course, but it begins with us. What a great feeling of accomplishment we would have if we were able to hire our own, build with our own, buy from our own, own our own!

Black folks need more black radio and television stations so that we can report the news as we see it. One could not help but notice that during the great debate of the latter part of 2000 involving the presidential election and the recounting of ballots in Florida, CNN, FOX, ABC, NBC, CBS and all of the other stations with the exception of BET were reporting the news from the white man's standpoint.

They gave Rev. Jesse Jackson very little time. They gave Rev. Al Sharpton and Minister Louis Farrakhan no time at all because they knew that these men possess the charisma to fire up the black spirit and they will tell it like it is. White folks are skeptical of black folks that call a spade a spade. We need reporters that will call a spade a spade.

Predictions For 2003 And Beyond

As crazy as it may sound if the United States defies the United Nations' advice and bomb Iraq we will find ourselves in a major war before the end of 2003. If things don't change in America we can expect a major civil war here in our country by 2005. Many black folks are getting fed up with the system. The whole system is corrupt.

I mean the whole system from welfare reform to the dismantling of affirmative action. Black folks are tired of witnessing the passage of laws that are aimed particularly at black folks. Black folks all over America are keenly aware of their God-Governed rights. The more intelligent a people become the more they will demand their rights.

The system is set up so that blacks can be seen as the minority. The percentages that you see in the census is made to look that way so that white people will benefit from jobs, grants and monetary distributions. Black folks are not crazy we know that we make up more than 13 percent of the population. I would estimate that blacks make up at least 30-40% of the United States population. We will never hear that from white folks because that would mean that we stand a good chance to win the white house.

It is estimated that in Houston Texas alone the census undercounted 200,000 people. They were all minorities. How many other cities and states have they undercounted in? Black folks should send their money and prayers to Dr. Cornel West,

Dr. Marcia Dyson, and the others who are on Rev. Al Sharpton's exploratory committee. I am very happy to see Rev. Sharpton run for president. I truly believe that he can win. I would like to see Rev. Sharpton choose Tavis Smiley as his running mate.

I believe that on one hand the younger generations of this day will reconcile with one another and will begin to treat one another the way that people should treat one another. In America today everything has a racial overtone and no race black or white is willing to give any ground. America is waging a silent war between blacks and whites this is a war that is not waged with sticks, stones or mortar. This war is being waged with subtle discriminations, prejudices, biases and racism. White folks to keep blacks out of mainstream American politics and economic decision-making have used these vices.

It is important to note that when the Klan has terrorized at its worst, it has always concerned the black vote. If blacks make up so little of the population in the United States and they do not have the power to affect the outcome of elections why did the Klan go berserk and threaten to kill without mercy those blacks or whites that tried to have blacks registered to vote?

Harry Moore and his wife Henrietta Moore of Mims Florida were both brutally killed by the Klan in Mims, Florida in 1951-1952 by the Klan because of Mr. Moore's fight for equal rights for blacks in Florida. The three civil rights workers that were killed in Mississippi were killed while trying to register blacks to vote.

If things don't change dramatically America is in for some dark days ahead. We live in the richest nation in the world. Yet, many elders are forced to choose whether they will eat properly or buy the medication that they need. We have tried to settle the drug problem in America with incarceration. We know that we are losing the war with drugs and despite our knowing this we continue to pack the jails with people who are only guilty of having drug addictions.

There are to many black families that are being broken up. There are to many adults that are spending countless number of years behind prison bars unjustly. We are presently spending over 640 billion dollars a year on criminal justice, to apprehend, process and warehouse prisoners in America and I think that this is ridiculous. Today 1 in every three blacks in America between the ages of 18-35 is under some form of incarceration or supervision of the criminal justice system, this is very disturbing to say the least.

Steps to Improve Multiculturalism in the Melting Pot

#1. We must first of all realize that we are not all the same. Our pigmentations in our skin are different yet we have the same body organs. Our blood pumps through our bodies the same. We all live and die the same way. Despite all of this we are still not the same. To be quite frank with you no one on earth is the same. We are all guilty of making statements that cause us to make generalizations about others.

Because we are all different we all possess different attitudes, morals, judgments, and prejudices. We eat different foods. We wear different clothes and hairstyles. We have different physical characteristics and intellectual capacities. We have different beliefs and affections. Last but not least we have different economic statuses.

We are not the same. No two people are the same. When we realize this fact we will not generalize as often as we do about each other. Black folks are not referring to just one white person when we say that white folks are doing us wrong. We make generalizations and say that white folks are dirty and no good as a whole. We do not take under consideration that just because one white person made us mad and may have fired us from our job, or asked us to be quiet in class, or suspended our kid from school, reposed our car etc. that does not mean that all white folks are lowdown dirty and no good. Depending on the circumstances that caused these actions to arise these white folks make not be low down and dirty at all.

We cannot make generalizations from one overt act or even a few acts and categorically say that all white folks are not good, that is not right. White folks must also realize that just because they encounter black men standing up and speaking out against racism that should not lead them to believe that he is racist or a troublemaker. When our comfort zones are challenged we should not resort to excommunication. If what is being said is true we should resort to change. White folks must not assume that just because their grandma's purse was jacked by a black brother, that does not mean that all black men are no good lazy, good for nothing, slouches, who want something for nothing.

This may have happened to your grandmother, your aunt and her sister in the same week but that still does not justify making generalizing that all black males are the same. It is never right to label the whole mass for the actions of the few. We must realize that we are not the same and that each race and culture has differences.

White folks love hockey, car racing, bungee jumping, skiing, mountain climbing and golf. I view these activities as being activities for white-men. Most black folks do not like high heights. Black folks are skeptical of anything that takes them to high in the air. I concur with D. L. Hughley who said on the Kings of Comedy tape that bungee jumping is too much like hangings. Most black folks are not about to let someone tie a rope around them and push them off of a bridge. I don't like flying much myself. Many black folk do not like sports that require you to use water or being in a cold environment. We are tropical people. We also don't like sports that require us to pay fees at country clubs.

We are different yet we are the same in many ways. If white folks and black folks are going to get along with each other in this 21st century we must be willing to recognize each other's differences and respect each other's feelings.

#2. The second things that we must do if we are to get along with one another is remove skepticism from our prejudice minds. We must not be suspicious of one another. We have always believed and been trained to believe that all people have ulterior motives for everything that they do. Why is it so hard for black folks to trust white folks and for white folks to trust black folks? I know that life teaches us to be skeptical.

I mentions Asian Americans in this book very seldom, yet they have made black folks in America feel very uncomfortable. It doesn't matter whether you are in California, New York, Louisiana or North Dakota, when black folks enter into Asian stores most Asians look black folks up and down as if they know that black folks are about to steal something. White folks don't even do that. White folks may say in their mind Lord help us when black folks walk in their stores but they very seldom follow black folks up and down the isles of the store.

It was refreshing to see more blacks collecting data for the census in 2000. When black folks see white folks coming to their houses to collect information they automatically become Skeptical. When blacks see other blacks coming to collect information they are still skeptical because they are trying to figure out is their any way that this information can be used against them. Let's be for real. There are thousands of black folk who do not want to fill out the census because they may have a warrant out on them. My stepfather always told us not to fill out the census because white folks were just trying to find out where all the black folks were at so that they could drop a bomb on us. I was a child when he said this but I still remember.

There are many black folks who have outstanding warrants, owe for child support, have traffic fines that have not been paid, owe the government taxes and education loans, are on the cities most wanted list. I am saying that we should be less skeptical about each other when there is no reason for our skepticism.

#3. Take a person at his word unless he/she gives you a valid reason to not take their word.

#4. Don't hold grudges against each other.

#5, Learn to forgive and try to forget.

#6. Encourage peace and cohesion not separation and discard.

#7. Be open to constructive criticism. Allowing open discussion and dialog on issues that may not be comfortable to you. Discussing these problems in a problem-solving manner with hopes of rectifying the problem and not merely discussing problems to get our points across.

#8. Commingle with one another make it a part of your schedule to visit a person or couple of another race at least once every three months. Take folks of other races out to dinner or invite them to dinner at your home. Allow your children to commingle with children of other races. Let your children know that we can accomplish much more by working together than we can by staying apart.

#9. We should allow others to identify our deficiencies.

#10. White folks should admit that slavery was wrong and pay each black person $100,000. Not each black family but each black person. Some folks may say they don't want a handout. Many black folks including myself would say to them I'd take your share.

Coming together in the new millennium.

As we embark on 2003, it is hard to imagine black folks and white folks living in a world together without coming together. There are a few things that must happen in the near future to ensure the survival of the races. The first thing that must happen is the coming together of the races. The race question is still the question of the 21st century. Racial Prejudice and racism can no longer be sweep under the rug. There must be answers to the questions and concerns of black folks in America if there is to be any peace.

My feelings are genuine and are meant to enlighten not to offend. This book was written in hopes of bringing races together and allowing the white man in America to understand how black people in America really feel. Beneath the skin of black folks is a book that deals with issues that black folks encounter day-to-day. Of course black folk smile in white folk faces, that is common sense, for it is from the white man that black folk receive their paychecks.

There are many situations in which black folks would like to voice their opinions. Most black folk feel that if they voice their opinions they will encounter repercussions and consequences. That is why they hesitate about visible protest or filing grievances.

Many of my friends have lost jobs because they filed grievances against someone in the system that was in the click. White people do stick together. A black man in many instances will file a grievance and be told that something will be done about the problem and something is usually done. Soon employers begin to find fault with the person that filed the grievance. Employers will then begin to gather documentation on the person that filed the grievance. In other words the norms that were accepted before the grievance was filed is now unacceptable.

Employers begin to document every time that person is late, any complaint he receives from other employees, or anything they do not complete or do on time. Black folks are then given a final warning and terminated.

The problem with all of this is that you knew that it was coming and there is usually nothing that you can do to stop it.

Dirty-Dirty

I have a friend who was a state trooper. He voiced his opinion and filed a grievance against someone on the force for making racial jokes. He was dismissed from his duties. Prior to filing the grievance this gentleman maintained an immaculate record with the department. His firing was a result of outright racism.

Many times black folk are aware of what is going in the system. Black folks know that white folk are not going to give them the promotions that they deserve. Many times white folks will hire someone that they know who is less qualified then blacks and make that person their boss. Once trained by black folks on the job, white folks will say that this person is better qualified.

Still We Rise

Many black folks feel that white folks do not want them to do better than they are doing. Black folks feel that white folks try to dissuade their progress. Yet in the words of Maya Angelou, still, we rise! Despite all of the unjust deeds that black folks have suffered at the hands of white folks, still we rise.

Despite the painful realities of segregated schools, pools, and separate fountains still we rise! Despite being served at the back door, still we rise. Despite the terrors of the Klan, still we rise. If none of these things stopped us in the past when we were not enlighten with the knowledge that we have now, there is no way that any race will stop us in the future.

If white folk intended for black folks to stay in the place from which he came, then they should have kept him in the position that he was in.

Rev. Nat Turner

White folks received an indication that black folks were not satisfied a long time ago through Rev Nat Turner. Rev. Turner felt that his mission from God was to free his people. Nat Turner led an insurrection in South Hampton, Virginia that made rattled the conscious of the nation.

No matter how black folks smiled and pretended to be happy, they were not happy. How appalling, for whites to believe that slaves were happy, how can one be happy, hoeing cotton from can't to can't? Can't see when you go into the cotton field because of the time of morning and can't see when you leave because of the time of the night. How ridiculous. Plantation owners were quick to brag that their slaves were obedient and content. Slaves were obedient because trying to escape meant having a limb amputated or being lynched.

Slave owners used escapees as examples for other slaves who might try to escape.

Today white folk are not allowed to whip black folks with whips. They can no longer drown, tar and feather, hang, burn, or mutilate black folks.

White folks use the legal system to keep uppity and troublemaking niggers in their place today. When black folks

97

speak out the local, county, or state police usually investigates them. If they are really speaking up, the Federal Bureau of Investigation investigates them. White folks will set out to silence radicals real quick. They will use the media and any other outlet to help them do their dirty work. Many people's lives and careers have been ruined because they spoke out about racial injustice. That is wrong.

Jesse's Troubles

During 2001 the media focused more and more on Jesse Jackson. They were labeling him a demagogue and a race baiter. The media said that he was stirring up trouble among the races. They were putting a bad rap on Jesse. I wondered why? It does not take a rocket scientist to figure out that white folks were mad at Jesse because he told black folks to stay out of the Bushes. He asked for and received 90% of the black vote for Al Gore.

Many white folks are mad at Jesse Jackson and they will do anything in their power to bring him down. I wrote in 2000 that I would not be surprised if Jesse was indicted in the next year or so on some trumped up charge that would be used exclusively to quite him down. I said that it might be income tax or anything, but I felt that they would try to find something on him. I did not know that they had already started an investigation.

White folks acted like they did not know what was going on. Like this just happened. Once again this was a prediction but black folks are not crazy we know what white folk will do and what they are capable of doing to a man that stand up and be a man. A real man who will not bow, break or bend!

This is especially true when you don't embrace or share white folks ideologies. I say to Jesse, I loved you from the start. I admired you in the beginning. Black folks in America love you very much and pray that the day will come when we all can march hand in hand with you and become spokesmen for human rights.

Rodney King

The climate for revolution in America is becoming much more apparent as each day passes by if things don't change. We saw what happen in Los Angeles when white police officers were acquitted in the Rodney King Trial. Black people were mad and they had every right to be. The white jury said to us that what we saw on the camera was really not happening the way it seemed.

Cameras don't lie. They may not always take pretty pictures, but they do not lie. Will there ever be peace and equality in America? I pray and hope so for the younger generation's sake. Many of us have been exposed to the good life now. When we didn't know any better, we were not expected to do better. Now that we know better, it is time that we do better. We have been exposed to freedom and a better way of living. Beneath this skin, we not only want this new way of life, we now demand it. Can we come together? Of course we can, but things must change. Personally, I would like to see the Government guarantee jobs for every American in America. I know that we have the resources to accomplish this goal. Instead of importing everything from overseas, why not produce many of these things here in America and give jobs to the people here.

Labor may be cheaper in other countries but the people of America pay a much higher price for decisions to produce goods in other countries.

Capitalism has great meaning and weight in American culture. If all Americans were employed receiving decent wages and every person that was willing to work had a job, black folks would have no problem embracing capitalism.

If individuals work harder than other they should receive more but receiving more should not serve to create a monopoly on other goods and services. This person's wealth should in no way prevent others from having the same opportunity to live the American dream.

It takes money to make money and for liberal republicans to say that poor people can do the same things that rich people are doing if they get off their bottoms is absurd. Republicans believe that black folks should be able to do so much with so little. If we could have them donate their salary to a poor family it would be interesting to see them pull themselves up by their bootstraps.

When white folks are put into similar position as black folks they begin to understand quickly why black folk are always frustrated, mad, angry, disappointed, skeptical, doubtful, rebellious, and on the edge. If white folks continue doing the same things they will continue to get the same results. If white folk want things to change, then they must be willing to change.

I have never been one to side with white folks with ease. I have never been one to say that it's the black man's fault that he is in the shape that he is in. Black folk did not pay their way to come here. They did not sail here freely. They were forced into this situation. Black folk were bought here against their will and now America must deal with what she has created in the black man.

Newsflash

I hate to say it but I told you. It was on last week that I predicted that soon or later they would come up with some story on Jesse Jackson as they have in the past with other black leaders that have stood up and spoke for black America. Americans are very devious. If white folks believe that you are commandeering and possess the power to have masses of people rally behind you, you are automatically considered a threat.

The story that broke this week about Rev. Jackson's extramarital affair that produced a two-year-old daughter came at a very interesting time. It happens to come right on the eve of the inauguration address of the new president and in my opinion did not come by accident. This is just another way that white folks tie black folks hands behind their back and render them helpless. African Americans view this as racism and in our minds it is further evidence of the great racial divide. Anytime a black man speak up and tell it like it is without scratching his head and looking at his shoes, white folks consider him an uppity nigger. White folks believe that black folks of this sort must be stopped by any means necessary.

Marcus Garvey

When Marcus Garvey started the UNIA (Universal Negro Improvement Association) in Harlem New York and masterminded a great uprising among the black people of America, the white man accused him of mail fraud. Garvey was sent to prison in Georgia for mail fraud. He was released from prison after serving two years. Garvey was released from prison but ordered to leave the country and never return again.

Martin King

Martin Luther King was shook to his foundation by the same kind of scandal. J. Edgar Hoover secretly bugged King's hotel room and recorded a possible sexual encounter that Martin had with a white woman. The CIA threatens to send the tape to Martin's wife and expose him on television if he did not shut up.

White folks meant to prove that King was a liar and a farce. These threats did not stop Dr. King and he continued to speak about racism and injustices that Negroes suffered at the hands of white folks in America. Every day that I live I witness new things. I can clearly see racism that exists on frontiers that were once foreign to me.

President Clinton (The Great)

The news media is the fourth form of government. They have talked about the outgoing president so bad this week until they have made people who did not like him to begin to like him. It is very plain to see that the media do not like President Clinton. Many white folks do not like Bill Clinton and Rev. Jesse Jackson. I was surprised to see Oklahoma Republican J. C. Watts Stand his ground with Bill O'reilly and not scorn Jesse. Deep down inside there is a special link between Watts and Jesse regardless of his personal views and his party affiliations. Watts realized that he and Jesse share a common brotherhood. They are both black folks.

Jesse's Woes

In addressing the issues that Rev. Jackson has encountered, I know that what he did was wrong. Who am I to judge him? I to am an ordained minister and pastor with many skeletons in my closet.

103

I want everyone that read this book to feel me and feel me right. It matters not if you are locked up, free, married, single, divorced, widowed, rich, poor, black, white, Republican, Democrat, employed, unemployed etc. I want you to understand that, what President Clinton, Rev. Jackson, Rev. Swaggert, Henry Lyons, Jim Baker and the list goes on and on has did is a common thing among politicians and the clergy. The only difference between them and other pastors and politicians is that the others have not gotten caught.

Tiger Woods, Venus and Serena Williams

Speaking on the behalf of black folks, we are proud of you. Now, I know how it felt for black folks all over America when Joe Louis knocked out Max Schillings and when Jackie Robinson broke the color barrier in professional baseball. We are proud of all of you and every other African American athlete who has represented black folks and when against the grain to become trailblazers opening doors for other African Americans.

American Made: Evolution Of A Dreamer (How I became who I am). Academics

From the eighth grade on up I have always been a member of the National Honor Society and various academic clubs. Many of my friends in high school and college often asked me how in the hell do you make good grades and we never see you study.

The fact is and was that I did not study. Not much anyway. I credit God with blessing me with slightly above average intelligence. It has never been hard for me to maintain a decent grade point average.

However, if you look at my report card from first grade I made almost all A's and B's the whole year. In the second grade my grades were C's D's and F's. I failed that year. I knew very well why I failed that year. I failed because I did not do my work. Playing with my friend Dreffus was more important to me than school was at this time. When I realized that I had failed and my other friends were leaving me behind that was all that it took to get me on the right track. Momma never had to worry about me from that period on. School has always been a very enjoyable experience for me. I have a great passion and love for learning even unto this day.

Integration

In 1971-72 when I was ten years old, they began to integrate the schools in Crowley, Louisiana. I remember a classmate name Russell, a white boy. Russell looked very funny to me. He had a square box head. His hair stuck up in the middle like Alfa-Alfa and he smiled a lot. Russell was from Morse, Louisiana a small country town located near Crowley. He was bused into Ross Elementary during integration. I grew up for several years believing that Russell was from the planet Mars because Morse was pronounced as Mars. I would ask Russell where was he from and he pronounced Morse like Mars. I always believed that Russell was an alien from outer space. It was quite a while before I realized that he was from another town and not another planet.

I also use to believe as a child that when stores closed in the evening that people would take their products home with them. As a child I was very inquisitive and wanted to know very much. My mother did a great thing when I was young that increased my curiosity and intelligence. She purchased a learning game that had questions and answers in science, social studies, geography, math, history etc. it came in a big box. You would select a sheet and put it in the game and push the lever and it would ask you a question and there was another card that had the answer on it. That game really helped me out in my school years.

When my nieces had baby-dolls some of my friends and I played with their baby dolls. I can remember asking my momma to buy me an easy baker oven. I was not gay, I just wanted to cook me something. I have dressed up in my momma's pumps and put on her wigs and make-up. We would have her purse clutched in our arms. That was fun to us. My brothers and nephews would do the same things, yet I have never been gay or wanted to be gay.

I think that we jump to conclusions to quick about things like that. I also had a lot of help from my brothers while growing up.

They always took time to help me with my homework if I needed help.

It was also in the third grade that I first fell in love with a teacher, her name was Ms. Butler my homeroom teacher. I had a serious crush on this woman. I daydreamed of she and I getting together more than I did my work in her class. Ms. Butler is probably around sixty years old today. During that school year she transferred to another city and school. My heart was broke. She even paid a visit to my house personally to let my mother and step-daddy know that she would no longer be my teacher. I was devastated. Man she was young and beautiful and I was in love! I don't remember who was my teacher after that but life went on and I moved on.

When I was in the sixth grade, I met a teacher who really tried his best to encourage me to become a Lawyer. His name was Mr. Simon but we called him Mr. Seymour. He was an older white male very nice and polite. He always tried to do his best in preparing his students. One day during a test he said that he noticed how I was going back over the same passage several times looking for details and he said those skills would aid me in becoming a very good lawyer if I chose to enter that field.

Jr. High

When I went to Jr. High I started playing sports. I had already played little league football for the bobcats and liked it. I also played for the colts.

It was during my little league years that I met two twins the Robicheaux brothers. I think their names were Tony and Troy. Those two white boys would chase me every day after practice. I think that they were just being mischievous more than anything. But the youth center was across the track in the white folks part of town so when practice or a game was over I got up out of there quick, fast and in a hurry. Today one of these brothers is the head baseball coach for a University in Southern Louisiana.

I tried out for boxing one year but when I saw the way that some people would get knocked out in the ring I decided to stick with football. I played little league tee-ball and was pretty good at it. But I never felt comfortable having someone throw something at me that fast and that close so baseball was out.

The game that I love even unto this day is football. Football has always been my favorite sport. In the seventh grade I did not play any sports but in the eighth grade I played every sport, football, track and basketball. I also met another teacher who I really admired very much during this time her name was Ms. Manuel she was young and right out of college. She helped me very much while I was a student in her class. When she would come to my desk and help me she always said kind words to me. Man I needed a lot of help in those days.

During my eighth grade year I was placed on the National Honor Society. This was the first year I was on the National Honor Society. My brother Rock (Percy) sung feelings the year before when I was in the seventh grade before the entire school body. Percy has always been able to sing. He was the lead singer for the Andrus Four.

High School

In 1977 it was off to high school. I was in the ninth grade. I felt good. I had finally reached the top where my other brothers were.

My mother has always been a staunch believer in education and wanted all of her children to finish school. I believe that nine of my mother's twelve children received a high school diploma and two completed at least bachelor degrees in college. My brother Walter received a degree in Psychology from Southern University in Baton Rouge in 1976. He was commissioned into the Navy as an Officer upon his graduation.

During my freshmen year in school I was into girls, sports and alcohol. My friends and I would sit around and just shoot the breeze. But it was not very long before I realized that I needed a job.

I was a model student in the ninth grade I did my work, played sports and obeyed the rules. I enjoyed my English teacher Mr. Dejean who would read Edgar Allen Poe's short stories. Man he scared the hell out of me with these stories especially the one about the Monkey's Paw. Mr. Dejean was always cool and I learned a lot in his class.

When I entered the tenth grade my principal was grabbing us and smelling us on the sly. He would come real close to your face and shake your hand, but he was really sniffing you for alcohol or drugs. Their were many days he must have had a cold or his nose was stopped up because if you looked at our eyes you knew we had been smoking or drinking. Later they started using dogs to search our lockers for drugs. Man school was crump.

School was school but it was also a social gathering for us and we would talk about the girls that we had hit the day before.

I enrolled in chemistry in high school and my teacher's name was Mr. Walker. He was a short heavy white man in his 50's. He set on a table one day and as part of an experiment allowed all of us to put our fingers under the table and lifted him up. We held him off the ground for several minutes with ease. I became a member of the Science Club because of that experiment. I was very fascinated with what I saw and learned in Mr. Walker's class. It was a very interesting year for me because it was also during this year that I met a girl named Susan.

Susan

Susan was from Texas and had come to live in Crowley with her grandmother. Man she looked very good to me. One day I asked her for her number and she gave it to me. Man I couldn't wait until school was over so I could call that chick. I fell in love quick. I wanted to be with her day and night. I probably would have quit school if she asked me to. I was in love for real for the first time. Susan and I kicked it for the next three years. We had each other's names put on our shirts. We were always together. Two of my friends started tripping with me because I was not hanging out as usual with the boys but who cared? I was in love!

One day after a school dance Susan and I went to my house to be together and I heard a laugh and my boys Don and Fred hollered my name and they took out running. They were listening to our conversation by the window that was cold-blooded.

We were Hebrews but this was my main-squeeze and they knew better than to insinuate anything that would mean an automatic whipping.

Susan was the sparkle of my eyes. As I think about it today, I believe that my relationship with Susan prevented me in many instances from getting into real serious trouble during my latter adolescent years.

Balling!

I had my own car that my step-dad had given me and I was balling out of control. I had a 1967 Bel-aire Chevrolet. Time passed by quick and before I knew it I was a senior. I still believe today that our senior class was the best class that has ever graduated from Crowley high school. We were the bomb and we knew it. Some of the girls that really got my attention in our senior class were very close to me. We had a great four years together. Egbert, Burnest, and Bubbie graduated a year ahead of us but the bulk of the Hebrews graduated together.

"Gone But Not Forgotten"

We did not have many fatalities in our class. I only know of one brother who was so nice to everyone in school who perished in our class shortly after graduation his name was Edward sparks, a very good friend of mine. He died in a car accident. Later, I attended the funeral of a very good friend and football team member Peter Batiste. Big Pete (Putt) was no joke. He was number 71 on the football team at Crowley High School.

Last year in 2002 we lost another classmate, Zelda Ceaser. Zelda was a very good friend of mine.

I also attended the funeral of Wayne Connelly my neighbor and friend. Edward, Dewayne, Zelda and Peter are greatly missed by our class. The class of 1981. I am sure that there may be others that I am not aware of and if so, they will be missed also. There are some guys like Donald Benjamin and James Savoy that I have never seen since graduation. When graduation approached it was nothing but a stone cold party and the place that we partied at was still Third Street. Everyone knew that when someone asked the question " What's the word"? The response was always third. That meant that the party was at my house. My house was located at 315 Moore Ave on Third Street. Our graduation was off the chain and after graduation we partied all night long. We were the youth of 1981. Today we have different kinds of youth.

Black Youth of 2003 " It Takes a Village"

Today our youth wear bagged pants hanging off their buttock showing their boxer shorts with one hundred and twenty seven dollar Air Jordan Nike tennis shoes. These youth wear expensive Polo shirts. They are clad with gold and platinum teeth, faded haircuts and they like to party. Many of these youth become discouraged because they cannot find work and they resort to selling drugs such as crack or marijuana. These youth are dealing with a serious crisis and if we fail to recognize their needs they are destined for trouble. We must realize that all children are different and that we cannot group all children in the same category.

I'll be the first one to admit that the youth of today are not the same as the youth of the 50's and 60's. However if we are truthful we will also admit that the youth of the 50's and 60's are not the same as the youth of the 20's and 30's. All of us have had our own time and as times have changed so have the people. We relate to norms that are practiced by our families and social structures.

Gold Teeth + Nice Cars + Loud Music = Arrest

My oldest son has four gold teeth in his mouth. My only concern for my son is the police. When police officers see a young black male with gold chains and gold teeth he is automatically a suspect or a dope dealer. I know that when black kids are flossing with gold chains, Spree-well Rims and a nice ride the police react as if this is drug related.

I am convinced that the youth of today are good-natured people who demand our attention. We should spend quality time with our children. We can do this by taking them fishing, hunting to a ball game or whatever they like. We should attend their games and take interest in their interests. When we spend quality time with our children they believe in us. They develop bonds with us that make them more accountable. When children know that you believe in them and that you are really concerned about them they feel more accountable to you. They will try their best to make you proud and happy.

Cast Aways

On the other hand if no one takes an interest in these young people, never find out what's on their mind, never support anything that they do, don't care if they pass or fail, don't care if they do their homework or not, these kids often become rebellious. Rebellion occurs in many different ways. Rebellion to some kids may mean doing something that you forbid them to do such as having sex or going steady with a boyfriend or girlfriend. Some children began drinking alcohol, smoking dope and taking pills to get high as a form of rebellion. Some children run away from home or nag you about staying at their friend's house. They tell you that they have more fun over at their friend's house just to make you feel bad, insecure and question the environment that you have provided for them.

Other kids rebel by doing poor in school, or getting in trouble at school. There are so many ways that a child can rebel. Some kids rebel by taking an overdose or inflicting fatal wounds to themselves. It is very important that we listen to our kids and what they have to say.

What's On Your Mind? My Son

I make it a personal habit to talk to my kids about anything that they have on their mind. My oldest son always has condoms in his pant pockets and his wallet. I have explained the facts to him concerning HIV, teen pregnancy and other diseases. I hope that he would refrain from having sex, but being realistic, I know that once a kid taste of the forbidden fruit (sex) there is usually no turning back. So we must explain to our children the consequences of having unprotected sex. Not only what it will do to them but what it may do to their partner also.

As we proceed through the 21st century we must communicating with our youth. We must constantly remind them that certain things are all right and that everything that they do is not wrong. I believe that many kids and teenagers do not confide in us with delicate matters because we are not open-minded. We are still trying to compare their day and time with our day and time and that is way out of sync.

I hear a lot of people say that when they were young they did this and that and they were not allowed to do this and that. But when you check the record young ladies of yesterday were having babies at 12, 13, 14, and 15 years old. This was happening in the 40's, 50's, 60's and 70's and it is still happening today. What is the big difference?

If we want our children to change we must change. Some of us must change the way that we talk to our children. I hate to hear a mother curse a child. When we talk to a kid like this we are asking for trouble.

Endangered Species Young Black Males

Mothers and fathers please don't curse your children. Try to talk to them with a firm but gentle voice without the cursing. In my years as a pastor, I have encountered many kids that were labeled at-risk kids. To be honest with you any kid that lives in poverty is at risk, and that risk is compounded when you realize that many of these kids live solely in female-headed households. It is an American tragedy to have black boys grows up impoverished without a male father figure.

How can we justify spending trillions of dollars on a missile defense system that we know do not work and the children in our country are going to bed with not enough food to eat. Many of these kids lack proper Medicare, Medicaid, Insurance and Nutrition. They have inadequate living environments and educational facilities. Our priorities are mixed up in a dangerously sad way. My hope is to see these children and this nation rise above rhetoric. I have seen American politicians talk a very good game, but, no very little actions has put forth.

Drugs/Alcohol/ and gangs:

I have never been a cigarette smoker in my life. But I have smoked weed and plenty, plenty, plenty, plenty of it. I am not the president. I did inhale mine and held it as long as possible. The first time that I smoked wheat was with my brother (blob) and his friend (Piallette). We climbed up on the Mason's building facing the graveyard and smoked a joint. I was about 12 years old. I was high, on top of a building, it was at night and I was looking at the graveyard. I was tripping, things started moving, and I knew that I had to go home. My brother told me to smoke a cigarette and that would make me have a mellow high. He told me to hold the smoke in and swallow the smoke. I took a big pull and held the smoke in. That smoke almost killed me. I was coughing and wheezing. I could not catch my breath. I was through with smoking. It has never taken me a long time to learn from my experiences.

Drinking Beer

Throughout my eight and ninth grade years I started drinking beer with my friends. We would give the older guys money to buy us something to drink. We would drink our beer real fast. We thought that drinking fast and drinking the suds would give us a buzz. After a while drinking was our favorite pass time. By 1977 when I was in high school we were drinking every day, even during football season. We always headed to a house that my mother owned that no one lived in, but the utilities were still on and the telephone. I believe that momma kept things that way just in case she had to make a sudden move she would have a place over her head. My friends and I hung out there all the time. We drank alcohol listened to music and just chilled.

The Birth of the Hebrews

It was also around this time that we began to form our clique into a youth gang. We never referred to ourselves as a gang but in reality that is what we were. Soon we became the Hebrews in Crowley and our rival gang was the Outlaws. One guy could not make up his mind if he was an Outlaw or a Hebrew. I guess he was like Richard Pryor whoever was winning the fight that was whose side he was on. We never had any real serious injuries occur between each other. Most of our dealings resulted in fistfights. We had a hell of a group. Egbert, Fred, Don, Burnest, Chuck, Zeeb, Bubbie, James, Murrell, and a few more baby Brews. We ran a tight ship. We were the originals.

We use to sponsored dances at the dance hall and raised money. I still don't know what we were raising money for. I know we did a lot of drinking. The Outlaws always came to our dances because they knew the girls would be there. Their girls and our girls were there. Usually after the dance we would go to Ruby's

Café and get us a pork chop sandwich and talk about what happened that night. Those pork chop sandwiches were swinging. But there was one problem. Ruby's was located in outlaw territory.

Durwood

One night I had a fight at Ruby's with an Outlaw. I fought him and his brother. I knew I was a bad man. I felt that no one could whip me. My boys pumped my head up calling me Durwood. I still don't know where that name came from but I know it got me whipped real good one day.

Slaughtered

One day in the park a Hebrew and an Outlaw had beef about a female. I traveled alone as backup. We had been drinking Budweiser beer all evening in the park. I had my boy's slack, but there were about eight Outlaws. When we approached the graveyard they started mixing. My boy jumped ship on me and hit the graveyard. It was dusk dark the sun had gone down and that bud got me to running my mouth. This Outlaw and I locked horns. This was the same one I had fought at Ruby's but this time it was a different story. He whipped me good. There is no other way to say it. I was soak and wet. They were kicking me, hitting me from behind and doing everything else. They all got a piece of me that night. I got up from the ground and took off running in their direction. When I got close to them, I was going to hit the outlaw in the head but he turned around and I ran into his fist, ka-pow, I hollered, dam! That was the end of the fight he straddled me and said who is top dog! I said you top dog. That was the end, but only for that night. It was on now!

Revenge

The next morning we had an emergency meeting at my house. The topic was REVENGE! We strapped up with a shotgun, brass knuckles, num-chucks etc it was war. We caught one outlaw slipping, he started talking trash and we did him real bad. Our plan was to catch them one by one. One day when I was playing football at the high school, I noticed that a white man was constantly following me on the sidelines. I played all through the game before they told me that someone had called the school and made a death threat on my life. The caller said that they were going to shoot me at the game that night. I knew exactly who it was. I did some real dirty things to some of the Outlaws. One day we all decided to call a truce. We had a real big party at my house and all of the Outlaws and Hebrews came. We put our money together and bought a lot of liquor and weed. We had a blast. After that night we never had any major problems with each other. We gained respect for each other but we never hung out with each other.

Elders in the Hood:

My neighborhood was filled to capacity with knowledge. The elders in our community took time to explain things to young children. They showed you how to plant a seed and how to milk a cow and how to butcher a hog.

I remember elders like Papa Joe who would let us walk his big German shepherd dog. He never knew that we were making his dog fight other dogs. Mr. Pop-pee who lived next door from my house would always wear his tee shirts and smoke his cigar. He loved to smoke King Edwards. He always sent us to the store to get him some royal crown hair grease. We all wanted to go to the store for Mr. Pop-pee because he would give us a dime and sometimes 15 cents. That was a lot of money to us when we were young.

If my memory serves me correctly it snowed on the day that Mr. Pop-pee died. Mr. Leroy, Mr. Whitney McZeal, Mr. Green, Mr. Oribo, Mr. Joe Broussard, Rev. Burnett, Mr. Lenny Johnson, Mr. Horace, Mr. Miller, Mr. Robinson, Mr. Reed, and Mr. Jackson were some of the men in my youth that I still remember very vividly.

Mrs. Nonk, Dydune, Lizzie, Scochhnie, Thibodeaux, Connelly, MacDonald, Mama Jane, Lop Tee, Minix, Hunter, Burnett, Duncan were always elder women in my life whom I remember. These elders played a very dominant role in my life. I learned very much from these people. I would cut their grass and sit on the porch and they would tell me stories. Now that I am older, I wish that I could sit on the porch and talk to these people now.

Momma Jane must have been ninety years old when I was cutting her grass. She wore three pairs of stockings and was always covered up. She gave me three dollars for cutting her yard. Sometimes she gave me four dollars. That was big money for a 10 year old in 1972. I would cut grass all through the community and come home with twenty-five or thirty dollars.

Momma knew that I was serious about making money and one day she bought me a new mower from western auto. My momma had good credit with the white folks downtown. I continued to work hard and one day when I came home momma had bought me a new stereo from Morgan and Lindsey downtown.

Evolution Of A Dreamer: From the Cradle to College (The Beginning)

Early life:

The earliest thing that I can remember about growing up was a funeral that I attended. It was very dark and cloudy that day. People were dressed in black. Back in Crowley, La. Where I grew up funerals were very eerie. When the hearse passed in front of our house, momma would make us close the screen door and the wooden door so that the dead person's spirit would not come into the house.

We had a very large family. I was the youngest of 12. My mother had ten boys and two girls all of us did not have the same daddy but that did not matter we were still brothers and sisters. My mother has always preached to us about respect. Anytime mother was away which was everyday, she always made it clear that the oldest child at home was always in charge so if anything went wrong there would be no questions asked. Momma was very stern. All of my mother's life she has worked for white folks as a domestic cleaning their houses, washing their clothes, cooking their food, taking care of their children etc. She did all of the things across town that she did not have time to do at home.

Momma managed to buy her one car in her lifetime that I can remember. It was a red 1965 Chevrolet Bel- Aire. This car was very sharp. The person who owned the car before she did had only one leg. The car had been modified to accelerate by pulling the air conditioner vent.

I remember that car very well because momma would often time hide me in the back seat when she was going to work early in the morning. She would tell me to keep my head down until she was out of sight of any of the other children. My brother Michael who is now deceased said to me once that he do not remember me being around much when we were growing up, I told him I know!

Family Tree

My mother was born in 1928 in Mallet, Louisiana. Her mother's name was Mary Thomas Vallier and her father was Toussaint Vallier. I had a chance to meet all my aunts and uncles before their death except my Uncle Houston who died of cancer at a fairly young age.

My Aunt Ledia (Leja) lived in Vinton La. I sort of hated going to her house because we had to cross a very high bridge in Lake Charles to get to her house. Once we crossed the bridge, I knew that we were in for big fun. I would get to see my cousins Chubby and Denver-Lee. I knew that my Aunt Leja was going to send Chubby and Denver in the chicken coop to kill one or two of those fresh chickens. She always made us fried chicken and light bread. Man my auntie could cook!

She always treated us very well. My momma was her baby sister. I always listened to the way they talked to her. They treated her like a baby sister. I have always been use to seeing mama in charge and ruling the family like a patriarch. She never argued with her older brothers and sisters in front of us. Aunt Leja was a very outspoken lady. She was the first one to nickname me Chimpanzee.

Shed and her sister (Aunt Louise) said that I always had my mouth open and my tongue showing just like a monkey.

My cousin Billy Aunt Leja's son still call me pan-nee today. This is short for chimpanzee.

My mother's other sister Aunt Louise was definitely one of a kind. I loved all of my aunts to death but my aunt Louise was without a doubt the boldest woman that I have ever known. She took chimpanzee a little bit further. Aunt Louise bought a black monkey and put it on her porch. The monkey had a big red tongue. She would always tell me that is how I looked. My Aunt Louise was a beautician.

She would press these women hair with a straightening comb. She must have done a good job because the women kept coming back. I attended head start one block from Aunt Louise's house. Sometimes I was instructed to go there until momma came to pick me up.

My aunt always analyzed her bills and if anything seemed to be too high she always placed her complaint. She learned how to read her own gas, water and electric meters. She always knew much energy she had consumed. She was very brilliant. My Aunt Louise was married to Uncle Wesley. Uncle Wesley always stood by my aunt's side even when she became very ill and died. He has always been a very good Uncle.

My aunt was the first African American that I know of to move in the white folks town. My aunt said that when she moved into her new house the white folks in the hood came over to make sure that she was moving in for sure. My aunt said a few months later all you could see was for sale signs down the street.

My aunts always spoke their minds about things in which they believed. They did not allow children to see around them when they talked to each other.

The Greatest Momma In The World

My momma's name is Alice Andrus, but many people called her Shorty. Mamma is about 5 feet. Momma has those short arms. When she gripped that extension cord and grabbed one of your hands it was on. Momma could whip like no one in the world. She did not play. These folks today have spoiled these kids with this child abuse. If anybody was abused it was the children who grew up in the sixties and seventies. We lived by the African Proverb in our community. It took the whole village to raise a kid.

Any elder in the neighborhood could whip you. They would whip you make you get on your knees and wait for your parents to come home. When they allowed you to go home you didn't even want to tell your parents you got a whipping. You did not want them to ask you those famous words "what happened"? When you told them what happened they would you did you do it. If you said no then they would say, are you calling Mr. or Mrs. Whoever a lie?

That would lead to another whipping. If whipped in the hood by an elder it would be to your advantage to just let it ride. Black folks were different then. My momma worked very hard as a domestic. She even saved enough money to buy us a house. I don' know how long we had the house but I do know that it burned down before I was out of head start.

Momma never did remarry anyone after my father drowned. She dated men but never married any of them. I have never called a man daddy in my life. Some of these men treated momma bad to me. I believe that momma took a lot of mess from some of these men because they were helping out our family.

My Father who I never really knew

My father's name is Warren L. Andrus. The people in the neighborhood called him Frog because I was told that he was a good swimmer. I guess one can say that his nickname is an oxymoron because the cause of my father's death was drowning. It has always been the belief of my mother and my grandmother that my dad was killed by two boys who did not like the idea that my daddy was going with their momma. I was told that these two boys did not like the idea that when their mother received her check she would give my daddy her mother.

The rumor is that they beat my daddy real bad and threw him in the canal by the standard mill. They found my father's body on Dec 23, 1963, frozen in a small canal two days before Christmas. When my mother received news of my father's death, it is said that she split a door in half with her bare hands. My mother knew that my daddy fooled around on her and yet momma has said that my father was a very jealous man. Momma said that if she even attempted to look outside the door at times he would threaten to slap her. That may explain our violent tendencies that some of my sibling and myself share.

One-day momma's employer gave her some ettoufee. Momma said that my father ate all of the shrimp out of etouffee and threw the gravy out. Momma was so mad she stabbed my daddy almost directly in his heart. She said that her children could have eaten the gravy with some rice. As a result of this incident my momma was placed in jail for one night. This is the only time in my mother's life she had been to jail. She stayed overnight and was released.

My mother believes that her employers got her out of trouble. They owned one of the biggest businesses in Crowley. They owned Dore's Rice Mill. Momma never had to go to court. She was never officially charged with a crime. My daddy on the other hand, I am told spent a few months in Angola for forging a check. My mother said that my daddy did work at the rice mills in Crowley and that he was a very good father to his children. My father provided for his family but he was still a man. Many people say that my father was an excellent singer just like the others his other brothers and sisters. My Uncle Frank was a member of the Los Angeles Choir and recorded with Rev. James Cleveland.

Growing Up Poor and Happy In Crowley Louisiana

I personally do not believe that there is a boy in the U.S. or the world who had a better childhood than I did. We were poor, very poor, but we were very happy. Momma always made a way for us. I have never in my life gone to bed hungry because we did not have anything to eat. We didn't eat all of the premium delicacies of the time but we were strong and healthy.

We use to play games such as hopscotch, war, shoot marbles, shoot a bow and arrow, and shoot sling-shots (aka) nigger-shooter. We use to see who can piss the highest. We use to try to piss on the roof. We made trails through the woods with pieces of roofing tin. We caught bullfrogs, went craw fishing and fishing.

When I turned 12 years old my momma bought me a 410 shotgun and I started hunting rabbits. I became a very skilled hunter at an early age. It felt good coming home with five and six rabbits in my belt loops.

I remember a guy name Percy who would catch garter snakes and stuff them with cotton. We lived by the bamboo. Many people would come by our house to get a piece of bamboo so that they could make them a fishing pole. You had to be careful when you broke a pole because the skin from these cane poles could cut you just like a razor. I remember some of my brothers' friends hanging a dog in a tree when we were young.

I have always admired my big brothers and their friends. I guess one advantage that I had on many kids was the fact that my brothers were always around. My brothers protected me and gave me advice.

There were many kids in my hood and we all got alone just like brothers and sisters. I remember so many kids in the hood. It would be impossible to mention them all. We teased each other but not nearly as much as these kids of today.

Many of my friends came over to borrow sugar, flour, eggs, milk, etc. and it was no big deal. Today, folks have so much pride. Many folks would sit in their houses and starve to death before they ask for something to eat.

When our house burned down we had approximately 15 people living in the house. Our neighbors pulled together and we all stayed in different houses in the neighborhood. We stayed there until they added two rooms to the tool shed in the back of the house. That tool shed became our home.

We had thirteen children and two adults living in a two-bedroom house with a kitchen and a living room. Our living room was exactly that a living room. We had a bed in our living room. If there had been enough room in the kitchen we probably would have had a bed in it.

When we went to sleep there were toes everywhere. If you turned your head to the left you saw feet and toes and if you turned to the right you saw feet and toes. Some days it would be hot. We didn't have rugs on the floor. In one room you could see the ground because a board was missing.

When it rained we had leaks everywhere. It seemed that every time you put a bucket in one place it started leaking in another place. It came to the point where we just made sure the beds were covered. We mopped up the water after the rain stopped.

We did not have hot water until I was in the seventh grade. We would warm our water on the stove to take a bath. We had gas but not enough money to buy a hot water heater. Hot water heaters were luxury items in my neighborhood. When the wind was high the tin on top of the house would rattle. It sounded like the tin was coming off. When it was cold outside we did not have to go outside to know about it. We could feel the wind seeping through the cracks. We had more drafts in our house then the army had during the Vietnam War.

We were poor but my momma is still the best accountant that I know. When things were bad momma would pull money from everywhere. If we needed anything for school momma always came through.

What Doctor

People did not go to the doctor for everything when I was a child. I remember throwing my nephew Troy's boot into a field one day. Troy threw a screwdriver at me. The screwdriver became lodged in my head. My mother did not take me to the hospital. Momma gathered spider webs from the corners in the house and packed the web in the small hole in my head. The web stopped the bleeding almost instantly. When our noses would bleed momma would roll up a piece of brown paper bag and put it between our top lip and our gums. This paper always stopped our noses from bleeding. Our parents learned how to improvise. Today, if children get a scratch on them we are dialing 911.

Television Shows in the 60's and 70's

The television programs that I remember most were the Lone Ranger, Lassie, Petticoat Junction, Three Stooges, Lost In Space, The Adventures of Johnny Quest, The Land Of The Giants, Lucy, Little Rascals, Soul Train, Baretta, The Rookies etc. There was no cursing and definitely no sex overtones on most of these shows.

Clothes

The clothes that they wore in the late sixties and early seventies were sharp. My brother Willie T and John Wayne Zeno were two fly brothers. They wore maxis. When super fly came out everyone wanted to be super fly. They had cars with gangster whitewalls, Afros, chains and high platform shoes. They wore shirts with elastic in the back with tie straps hanging down. It was crazy but it was fun. The women had Afros, thigh high boots and big earrings. To top it off they were wearing mini skirts.

Initiation Hebrew

To be a part of the Hebrews in the late 70's was a great thing. Our motto was "Hey Hebrew, so what!" (In funk we trust)". We always clowned around with one another and made fun of each other. We spent hours laughing and telling jokes to each other. If you wanted to be a Hebrew there were some things that you had to be willing to do. Sometimes we would pull trains on girls.

Freaky Tales

We never raped any women. We always had their consent. Some young women would just take us one by one. We had one chick out of town that took care of all of us. We really thought that we were the bomb. I remember on one occasion being out of town and we were all about to get served. There were five or six of us on this particular day. My boys always joked saying I would be the last one because they knew once I hit it that was it. They use to laugh the night away talking about how the car was rocking up and down. They said man T tore it up. A few of my boys didn't let it end like that they went back for seconds.

One night we were at a house party and this girl sexed all of us. We were wide open and straight balling. Zeeb always teased me. They acted like I was horny and was not getting laid. They always messed with me, until I pulled one of the nicest looking girls in the school. I knew that even though I was a scrapper that would not stop my boys from trying to hit my girl. In my day holding on to and losing your girl was just part of the game. You won some games and you lost some games but you kept playing.

Initiation (What would you do to be a Hebrew)

One night we all were walking down the street and we decided to call each others bluff We said that if we are real Hebrews we should have no problem getting buck naked and walking down the street. That was the beginning of our initiation.

We stripped naked and walked about eight blocks. When we saw a car we would run behind people's houses. We left our clothes in a certain area so we had to handle our business to get back to our original destination.

One night we ran through the nursing home with only our briefs and a shirt. That became another part of our initiation ritual. We did some real crazy things when I was a kid. We were just finding things to do. We always challenged each other. We wanted to find out who could drink the most alcohol at one time and who could drink alcohol the fastest. We wanted to know who could take the longest charge of marijuana. We had one Hebrew who introduced us to black mollies. Black mollies were prescription pills. Those pills made your throat dry. I have never been to crazy about taking pills because it is hard for me to swallow them.

Juvenile Delinquents Without a Record

I remember one day riding with two of my partners just getting high. I told them to take me to my girl's house. They took me there but I could not get out of the car. I was so messed up. These guys instead of taking me home helped me out of the car. I fell right on my face and started throwing up. They just laughed. I was so embarrassed. I could not move. It was raining. That was all part of the game. I probably would have done the same thing to them so that we would have something to talk and laugh about later.

One day we all went into this clothing store on Parkerson Ave and the guy working that day did not seem to be that bright. We all took out our bags and nearly cleaned that store out. I feel bad about that now but at the time, we were just hitting folks up stealing clothes and shoes.

We would buy posters and have them put the posters in a large bag. We would discard the posters and enter the stores acting like something was already in our bag. We would fill our bags up with anything that looked good and was our size. We did not hesitate to take what we wanted.

One day we stole so many items from a department store we just gave the manager on duty all of his clothes back. I remember us stealing boots out of a store one day. Our homie was suppose to open the door for us once he got out the store because where we were the door did not open from the inside.

The windows were tinted and he could not see us on the inside. Man when he passed by us he passed up the door so I knocked on the window and man that dude took out running. When we finally made it to the outside thanks to someone else coming into the store we laughed like crazy. When the door opened we just walked out.

We all did things that could have landed us in reform school while we were young. Somehow, we managed to never get caught.

Smoked Out

In 1976 marijuana should have been legal. Everyone had marijuana and they use to sell large amounts for a little money. We smoked so much wheat at time seemed to not get us any higher. One day Regg sold me some killer wheat. The wheat I smoked that day was more potent than any wheat I have ever smoked in my life. Man that killer had me getting out of my car in the middle of the road. I felt like I was hitting the brakes and the gas at the same time. I was paranoid and tripping real hard. I just threw the gearshift up in park while the car was still running.

I was less than a block from my house and I could not even back up. When I stepped out of the car one of my brother's friends happen to be passing by and he said man was wrong? This guy was a twin, I don't know if it Bobby or Billy. I said man I can't drive this car. I asked him to drive my car home for me. I was talking like I was freezing but it was the middle of the summer.

I went to the Rick James and Tina Marie concert in Baton Rouge that weekend. I gave my girl a hit of that killer. I was scared of that smoke because I knew what it had did to me already. I was trying to be slick. My objective was to give her some wheat (reefer) and get her in the mood so we could do the nasty. She smoked that refer and I couldn't get her to shut up. She bumped her gums all the way from Baton Rouge. She was talking about the heat was slowly moving from her toes towards her head. I had messed up bad. Smoking wheat, drinking all kinds of alcohol, pulling trains, fighting, stealing, going to church, and being respectful to elders were a way of life for most of us.

A criminal Record

One day a Sheriff Deputy named Mr. Deville told my friend and I to take some trash out of his cans because his cans were not for public use. He said that his cans were for the use of his store only. Mr. Deville was a white man in the black neighborhood. I felt that the least he could do was let us discard our trash in his can. To make a long story short he made us remove the trash and that night after drinking a few cans of bull. My friend and I kicked the store's door down.

The first car to turn the corner was the police. I took off running. My friend a Hebrew went into the store. Mr. Ceaser who many people called Mr. Bo-Bo, caught my friend and took him in. The next day at school I was worried as hell.

The worst part of committing a crime and getting caught for me was having to break the news to my momma. I felt real bad because I had let my momma down. That really hurt me real bad because my mother had always struggled to give me her best. Momma provided for my sibling and myself. My friend's sister told me the next day at school that the police were looking for me. I was scared as hell. I went to the police department and turned myself in. My mother was with me. Man that really devastated my mother and myself. They gave my friend and I two years probation.

My probation was completed unsatisfactorily because I never went to see my probation officer and I never paid for the lock that we broke. This was my first felony and little did I know that it would not be my last.

There are many people who are charged with crimes and because they do not know the law that are railroaded. If my family could have hired a paid lawyer the most I would have received would have been probation. I would have not had a felony. I found out later that in order to be charged with simple burglary a person must enter into the premises with the intent to deprive the owner of his property. I did kick the door in but when it opened, I did not go in. I should have been charged with vandalism not burglary.

The beginning of the End

In 1989 I was arrested for check kiting charges. I had managed to open up several bogus accounts at several banks. My business was in trouble and I needed money. I had a choice either suffer embarrassment from losing my home and cars or check kite a few checks and hope that business would pick up. It was not hard for me to make my decision. I had grown accustomed to having money and I wanted the money and the fame that came with it. I deposited checks in bogus accounts and received large sums of money from banks. I had charges in Shreveport, La., Bossier City, La., Texarkana, Texas, and Houston, Texas. I was subsequently sentenced to concurrent 6 years sentences in the Louisiana and Texas. I was remanded to jail in March of 1991 and released in March of 1994 after serving three years.

During my three years of incarceration I worked as an inmate Lawyer at Wade Correctional Center in Homer, La. I was released with a superb prison record. I did not have any disciplinary rule violations. While in prison I had the pleasure of serving on the inmate welfare council, and in various clubs.

Home Sweet Home

After my release from prison in 1994, I worked for Rev. Huey P. Lawson, a prominent minister in Alexandria, La. who helped me out tremendously. My wife and two children moved to the

Bethel Apartment Projects in Alexandria thanks to Rev. Shaw an AME Pastor and Ms. D. Dudley.

I began to working for the Rapides Parish School Board as a Teacher's Aide at Reed Avenue Elementary in the same year. While working at Reed Ave. Elementary I met my future mentor, Mr. Julius Patrick. Mr. Patrick served as Mayor of Boyce, La. I decided to re-enter school but this time my focus was criminal justice.

I enrolled at Louisiana College, a private liberal arts college in Pineville, La in the spring of 1995. I was enrolled as a part-time student. I received my associate's degree in criminal justice in 1999 and my bachelor's degree in criminal justice in year 2000.

In the summer of 2000, I moved to Monroe, La. where I entered into graduate school at the (ULM) University of La. at Monroe. There I pursued my master's degree in Criminal justice. It was during this time that I received my first teaching job as a 665 teacher at Lincoln Elementary School. I will always be grateful to Mr. Roy N. Shelling the Principal at Lincoln Elementary School.

Pastor Andrus

While living in Alexandria I was pastor of Donahue Third Street Mission Church. The Southern Baptist Convention in Rapides Parish supported the church. The church was called Third Street Mission.

This mission church opened in February of 1996, after having started a congregation in an old funeral home in August 1995, I transferred my flock into the building donated to me from the Southern Baptist foundation. This building was used to build my ministry. When I first moved into the building Third Street Mission had approximately 26 members that attended on a regular basis. Two years later we had a membership of approximately 150 members and a vacation bible school that averaged at the least 400 students per day. I contributed my success in church building to my willingness to go out into the highways and byways and compel men to seek Christ.

Trouble on the Rise

It was in the same summer of 1998 that I was arrested on a Sunday evening while cruising in my Jaguar with one of my deacons. I was originally charged with speeding 40mph in a 25mph zone. I told the police officer that I was not speeding and that I was not going to sign the speeding ticket. The officer said to me that I was a smart-ass nigger! I refused to sign the ticket and I was placed under arrest. My Jaguar was impounded. The officers broke my trunk lock. The officers were still not able to gain entry into my trunk. They were looking for drugs, thinking that I was a drug dealer because I owned at the time 2 Mercedes Benz, a suburban and a Jaguar.

They did not realizing that I owned rental property in several areas of Alexandria that supplemented my income from the school and the church. En-route to the police station the arresting Officer accused me of threatening to kill him and his family. Later the other three officers said that I threaten to kill them also. I was charged with public intimidation of a police officer. If I had found guilty I could have been exposed to the Habitual Offender Bill and only the Lord knows how many flat years in Prison they would have given me.

Protest March

After posting bail I organized a protest march that bought out the black Muslims, my church congregation and other citizens who was sick and tired of being sick and tired. I was the keynote speaker at this rally. I sounded my horn real loud. There were over 50 police escorts in unmarked cars and motorcycles. We marched hand in hand with other demonstrators chanting no justice no peace. We sung Negro spirituals such as "we shall overcome".

This revolution begun in Alexandria and soon other black folks and white folks were making noise and staging complaints. An organization was formed in the black community called the POWER (people organized working for equality and righteousness). This movement was organized by local black ministers and became a force to reckon with.

Rev. Solomon Shorter and Minister Bryan Muhammad lead the movement. Rallies were organized and meetings were held in city hall where citizens could come forth and tell their story of how they were brutalized and mistreated at the hands of the Alexandria Police Department. I personally referred to the Alexandria Police Department as the most crooked, most racist police department south of the mason-Dixon line. Blacks and whites came out and told their stories of how they were abused at the hands of the Alexandria Police Department. We threaten to boycott the stores in the mall. I delivered the demands of the group to the Mayor of Alexandria, Ned Randolph. We demanded that he take action against the police department and the chief of police or there would be unrest in the city.

Before things could materialize a meeting was called and the officers in the Greg Hunter incident were placed on Administrative duty and we received promises from the city that we would have a citizens review board put in place. Therefore the boycott/protest was called off.

Trial For Public Intimidation

In June of 1998, I went to trial on the charge of public intimidation. I have never seen a courthouse so full of people. One side was filled with blacks. The other side was filled with whites. Almost every Asst D.A. in Rapides Parish was in the courthouse. They were there and I was facing in my opinion the most racist/prejudice DA in the United States. It seemed to me that this guy had something to prove. He wanted to prove to all of the white folks that he was going to get this nigger troublemaker off the streets once and for all. After all Tracy

143

Andrus had caused other black folk to question what was happening to them. They could not let this happen because that would mess up the go ole boy system that had been in place for many years in Rapides Parish.

They felt that they had to make an example out of me so that they could teach all the other niggers in Alexandria a lesson. Their lesson was don't don't mess with white folks because if you do you are going to lose! That was their plan. They had a win-proof strategy. They were planning on introducing my record as an ex-convict and show that I had previously did time in prison.

"Only God Can Judge Me"

The D.A. comprised a jury of 5 whites and one black. The judge was white. The four police officers were white. I felt like Moses and the children of Israel. I felt that I was surrounded on the left and right by the mountains. The sea was in front of me and the Egyptians were in the back. I know that if I was to be vindicated it would have to be by the hands of God because they wanted me to fall in that city.

My trial lasted for one week from Monday to Friday. It was about 6:00 Pm that Friday that the jury announced that they had a verdict. The court reporter read the verdict that said we the jury find the defendant Tracy Andrus not guilty of public intimidation. It seemed like all of the people in the black section had won a million dollars. We jumped, hollered, cried, hugged,

144

shouted and did everything that we were not supposed to do. The judge hit his mantle and pleaded for order in the court, but the way we were feeling we would have just paid the contempt fine. I was thanking my God who had saved me from my enemies. Attorney Ed Larvadain had represented me and did a very fine job. Attorney Larvadain had performed as if God spoke through him for my defense. I am grateful to Mr. Larvadain unto this day.

During the times that we were having altercation and protest marches, I received a call from the pastor of Donahue Baptist who said to me that I was creating to many waves for him by outwardly protesting against the police Department.

James Greer happened to be white and owned a very successful tire business in Rapides parish and elsewhere. He indicated to me that if I would not be willing to tone it down, I would be relieved from my duties as Pastor of Third Street Baptist Church, I said to him to do what he must but, I would never shut-up after suffering this type of humiliation at the hands of those who are suppose to be there to protect and serve. I was dismissed from my duties as pastor and filed a lawsuit against the church and the police department. I was later told that my statue of limitations had expired and that I was not entitled to compensation for any of the wrongs that were dealt to me. Yeah Right!

White Flight/Black Fright

I looked at his decision as I have viewed white folks all alone. They were looking out for one another as usually. I knew that I would have a snowball's chance in hell of winning the lawsuit, but I gave it my best shot. I knew that the police wanted me real bad. I decided for the sake of my family and my education to move to Monroe. Once in Monroe I attended ULM pursuing my master's degree in criminal justice.

The Developing Theory of Enviroecogenetics A Crime Causation Theory

"The Real reason Black Folks and Poor Folks Commit Crime In America"

By: Tracy Andrus

Abstract

If the explanation to crime lies in the blood of criminals (biologically or genetically) our only basic need, as humans would be to construct razor wire around the parameters of the earth because we are all criminals! Many positivists' criminologists have tried to predict future criminals by identifying certain external and internal physical characteristics to no avail. Delinquency and crime are the results of many factors, yet few factors weigh heavily on all criminals in the justice system. Enviroecogenetics identify three important causal factors of crime and delinquency.

One in five children under the age of 15 lives in poverty, and a staggering 50% of all black children under the age of six live in poverty in the U.S. Over the last 25 years black unemployment has remained slightly more than twice the rate of white unemployment. Among those in the crime prone ages of 16 to

19, 12.7 percent of white youngsters and 31.6 percent (more than one of every three) black youngsters were jobless.

In 1999/2000 there were more African American men in prison and jail (791,600) than were in higher education (603,000). Between 1980 and 2000, Justice Policy Institute estimated that 3 times as many African American men were added to the prison system than were added to the nation's colleges and universities.

According to the Bureau of Justice Statistics there were 1,965,495 persons in custody in federal, state and local jails in June 2001 (BJS, 2001). Between 1980 and 2000 the American prison and jail population quadrupled from 500,000 to 2 million prisoners (JPI, 2002). During the same time state corrections spending grew at 6 times the rate of higher education.

Enviroecogenetics seeks to analyze and explain and identify factors related to the high incarceration rates of impoverished juveniles and adults. Enviroecogenetics attempt to explain and contrast to what degree or extent does living environments; economic status and genetic predisposition determine criminality and delinquency. This theoretical hypothesis also seeks to explain among other things to what degree or extent does environment, economic status and genetic predisposition positively affect criminality and delinquency. Finally, Enviroecogenetics seeks to determine whether or not a person's genetic makeup predisposes them to crime and delinquency to a greater extent when his/her biological parents have been criminals.

Enviroecogenetics Theory further attempts to explain why crime and delinquency is present to a greater degree in impoverished neighborhoods. The positive factors identified by this theory include a person's living environment and economic status. The neutral factor identified includes a person's genetic makeup. This theory assumes that if criminal genes cause everyone in the human race crime then has the criminal gene because everyone is susceptible of committing crime.

Introduction

Enviroecogenetics affects all families regardless of social status, location, or ethnicity. These effects can be positive or negative.

This research article introduces a new perspective on crime causation while analyzing, critiquing and integrating various theoretical approaches to crime and delinquency. Sociologists, Criminologists, Psychiatrists, Psychologists, Penologists, has influenced the field of criminal Justice and compiled vast amounts of research. Many of their studies have overlapped into different disciplines. While Enviroecogenetics has much originality it also relies on research undertaken by various schools and theorists from the past. These theorists include people such as, W.E.B. Dubois, Monroe Nathan Work, E. Franklin Frazier, the *Chicago School* (Shaw and McKay), Edwin Sutherland (*Differential Association Theory*), Caesura Lombroso (*Positivist/determinist Theory*), Karl Marx (*Conflict*

Theory), Robert Merton (*Anomie Theory*), Nicole Rafter (*Eugenics Theory*), Coramae Richey Mann, William Julius Wilson, Darnell F. Hawkins, Vernetta D. Young, Walter Miller and Cloward and Ohlin's (*Subculture Theory*), Walter Reckless and Travis Herschi's (*Social Control Theory*), and Burgess, Ackers and Jeffery's (*Social Learning Theory*), and Becky Tatum.

Enviroecogenetics is a continuum of many of these theories with a present day interpretation.

Literature Review

(The Impact Of One's Environment On Crime And Delinquency)

Most theorists in the past have readily admitted that a person's environment usually help shape their norms, moral codes, world-view hypothesis and later views on life. A person's living environment is the most important contributing factor that will determine whether or not the person will develop behavior that is deem by society to be good or bad.

Middle Class Children Environment

Children who are born to parents, who are educated, financially stable, have access to conventional means and are able to adequately provide educational services are much less likely to get into trouble with the law. If these kids do get in trouble their parents have the means to free them from the legal system.

Living On the Brink of Disaster

Many families in minority communities are constantly living on the brink of disaster. Stress and pressure are tugging at the core of their thoughts from day to day. Children are exposed to the struggles of their parent(s) who is usually a single black mother living on the threshold of poverty. Mother usually does her best to provide for the children in the family, usually working long hard hours for minimum wages. While she is away from home there are periods of time that the children are left unattended, unsupervised or they are left in the care of others who are kids themselves. For their children so that they may accomplish their goals have a very low chance of becoming criminal or being charged and convicted for a criminal offense. These children are usually surrounded by middle-class, wealthy people who view success as the norm. These children grow up knowing that they will attend college. There is no question as to whether or not they will attend college their only concern is what college will they attend.

Evolution of Delinquency In Impoverished Environments

Many children begin to develop deviant behaviors at a very early age (Glueck, Sheldon, 1956). They repeat what they hear and what they see (Sutherland, 1939), (Shaw and McKay, 1942). Their environment affects them tremendously.

Many children see their mothers struggling day by day. They witness the lights and other utilities being turned off and their parents being evicted from the place that they have called home.

151

Often times these children find themselves having to constantly move from one place to another never really certain where they will be. These kinds of environments produce instability and shame in children. They meet new friends and develop relationships only to have to sever them at the time of eviction.

Environmental Impacts on Delinquency and Crime

As a result of the turmoil in the homes many mothers turn to unconventional means to make ends meet. These unconventional means may include prostitution, issuing worthless checks, boosting, theft etc. Impoverished women tend to put up with a half of a man (A man that she knows is married or have some significant other) who is willing to provide means of support even if he may be somewhat abusive verbally or physically. If many of these women were in better financial conditions they would not put up with these kinds of situations. Out of the necessity of, trying to keep the bills paid, keep a roof over the heads of the children as well as themselves and keep food on the table many single mothers are forced to tolerate situations that would normally be unacceptable.

Abuse and Misuse Matters

Often times the children of these single parents are exposed to the mental and physical abuses that their mothers suffer at the hand of the manta Claus (a person in your life that brings you happiness and discontent). When a person (single-mother) is forced to depend on a relationship such as this and the dominant partner is cognizant of his importance to the welfare and well-being of the dependent family, he usually exerts a don't care attitude that in many cases lead to physical, verbal and mental violence to the children and mate. This violence usually takes place in the presence of the children.

The dominant spouse in relationships such as these is more likely to have additional outside relationships and will usually not really care if either of them know about it and this will in most cases lead to confrontation.

Environment and the Evolution of Crime

Children living in environments such as these are constantly exposed to the many friends and relatives of their parent(s) that smoke dope, drink alcohol, gamble, curse, lie, steal, and do other things that warp their psyche and diffuse their cognitive abilities (Sutherland, 1939), (Shaw and McKay 1942). In the homes of these youth there are no set social values or conventional norms for the most part. If there are any conventional norms that are present they are very weak and unstable.

Inconsistency, Delinquency and Criminality

Grandmother may take them to church and talk about the lord, but even when she gets mad she uses profanity and talk about getting even with others in the present of the children. That does not coincide with what the children view as being expected behavior. This confuses the child.

Visions of Life outside of the Ghetto

Very early in the life of these children they realize that they do not want to live like their parent(s). Most parents who live in hostile environments that listen to their children quickly realize that their children's intentions are to do better than them when they grow older.

Young poor children fantasize about becoming professional athletes when they grow up because most of their role models are athletes and entertainers usually rappers. In order to understand why blacks behave the way that they do, one must understand the root cause for their thinking. Before one can understand Blackness, African Americanism, Negroism one must understand that living among blacks in any American community is a very different experience. Blacks are very unique and have deep-seated roots, ideologies, beliefs, customs etc. Children in very poor neighborhoods (black or white) do not see white-collar executives leaving from their homes every morning with their white shirts and paisley neckties driving their Mercedes, Lexus or Range Rover. That is why when poor kids especially black kids are asked what do they want to be when they grow up very seldom if ever say they want to be a businessman/woman. They want to be athletes or rappers because these are the ones from the ghetto that usually make it to the big time.

Life Without Struggle

These children have a great desire to live a life without struggle. As they grow older and reach elementary school they began to understand some of the realities of life. These children are at this time facing their first major status problem (Cohen, 1955). Most of these poor lower-class children are measured in school by the middleclass measuring rods, and when they are evaluated unfavorably they become frustrated (Cohen, 1955). These young men and women sense from their surroundings and their early experience that life is not going to be as easy as they once though that it would be. They neither began to realize through socialization at school that they are not the same nor treated the same as others who have what they don't have. Soon clouds of doubt begin to linger in their innocent minds and they feel spurts of inferiority settling in.

The Dark Cloud

These children began to question their potential about time they reach 2nd, 3rd or 4th grade. Soon many of them are faced with making life-changing decisions. Just like dogs, cats and any other creature who has the capacity to appreciate condemnation they are soon forced to make decisions as to whether they will stay in school or not. As they grow up many of these youth put in applications at various places and are never called some continue trying to make money through conventional means, but some youth get caught up with selling drugs and engaging in different hustles. They view these means as an alternative way to the top. This is usually a reaction to rejection (*reaction formation*) (Cohen, 1955), (Subculture Theory), Walter Miller, 1958).

The Bright Cloud

Most minority young men admire those who are successful in their community. Whether are not fame and fortune is obtained through conventional or unconventional means is not important to most of them. They just admire and want to have the nice Lexus, Suburban, Impala, Benz with the Datons, Sprewells or the hundred spokes dripping candy with the boom in the trunk, teeth grilled out, gold chains and rings with many women. Now that's the Average Young African American man's dream in America. These young people are not concerned about owning a piece of America.

Theoretical Assumptions

This theory speculates that crime can be reduced significantly if resources are allocated in impoverished communities to help rebuild and beautify the city's infrastructure that African Americans return to everyday. In addition to this increased economic support from governmental entities to improve the infrastructure African Americans and other impoverish classes must be given the opportunity to work and earn decent wages. Steady employment in impoverished neighborhoods would contribute significantly to reducing the crime rates of adult and juvenile offenders in impoverished communities. Research has indicated that the increase in crime rates in impoverished communities has resulted from the poor having inadequate means to acquire their goals. The placing of adequate means in impoverished neighborhoods would serve to facilitate the uplifting of the *Truly Disadvantaged* (Wilson, 1987).

Means such as Vocational schools, Technology schools, Banks, Credit Unions, Mortgage Companies, Clean Parks, Community Centers, Commercial Colleges, Universities, Large Chain Grocery Stores, Shopping Malls and other business entities, including Junior Colleges even if they are extension campuses in the black community are needed to help prepare and facilitate the preparation of the underclass. These sectors would prove to be detrimental to the survival and uplifting of impoverished communities. These institutions would provide avenues through which juveniles and adults can acquire conventional means to attain their goals.

This theory also assumes that the availability of jobs and proper medical services are interrelated with the causal factors that determine to a certain extent crime in the black community.

Studies in criminal justice that have tried to identify to what extent factors impacted crime have been hard to measure because most subjects that were being analyzed were not part of a controlled environment. Enviroecogenetics seeks to explain the co relational relationship of crime in regards to a person's living environment, economic status and genetic predispositions.

Impoverished Children Environment

Children born to impoverished families where parents are uneducated, living from paycheck to paycheck, have no expendable income, lack financial stability, lack assets to fall back on, do not have access to means that will help their children achieve their goals are more susceptible to committing crime and delinquency.

Researcher Bias

For researchers to say that disadvantaged impoverished children have the same chances for success as middle-class and wealthy children is absurd to say the least. A child's family structure and financial ability will determine how he/she is socialized to a great extent. People with money have the resources to put their children in private day care and learning centers where they are given constructive educational assignments and monitored closely, whereas the poor must leave their children with whoever is available to watch them. It is during the early years of a child's life when their cognitive abilities are most susceptible to learning that the middle-class and wealthy families are able to outpace the disadvantaged and poor in educational attainment. Researchers have indicated that mothers should begin reading and perfecting educational challenges during their pregnancies because children begin to learn while in the mother's womb.

The Plight of the Poor

Most Poor and disadvantaged parents cannot afford the luxury of sending their children to adequate day care centers because of the lack of finances. Many poor parents allow their children to be left with older children or friends whose primary responsibility is to make sure that the child has something to eat and that the child does not hurt itself. Exploring educational challenges is usually nowhere in the picture. As a result of not being in a structured environment where colors, shapes, phonics are taught the child suffers tremendously because of under development of cognitive functions.

Impact of Poor Environments

Many children of the poor are raised in environments that encouraged delinquency and opposition to conventional norms. Poor Children are socialized for the most part by grandparents, uncles, aunts, cousins and friends of the family who in many cases are marginally illiterate, abusive, drug addicts, pedophiles, or alcoholics. When parents are not financially able to select services for their children they must settle with doing the best that they can. The majority of people want what is best for all of their children, but because of the lack of financial stability and living in impoverished degraded environments impoverished kids are socialized differently from middle-class and wealthy children. These children of the poor grow up in different environment and learn different social values and norms. This is not to say that all kids from poor families grow up without proper manners, low IQ's or are destine to become criminal. However the chances of becoming delinquent or criminal increases with lower economic stability, unstable living environments and genetic predisposition.

The Contrast Between the upbringing of the haves and the have-nots (Rich and Poor).

The rich and poor are exposed to different environments that aid in shaping and developing their attitudes and beliefs about life and living in general. Most impoverished children are exposed to living in environments that are frequented with cursing, fighting, drinking alcohol, smoking dope, and gambling everyday to name a few external characteristics. Exposure to activities such as these by children affects their cognitive development in ways that later become a permanent part of that child's psyche.

Edwin Sutherland viewed crime as being a result of individuals following culturally approved behavior that was disapproved (and set in law) by the larger American society (1939:9). Sutherland further stated that differential association theory is entirely a product of the social environment surrounding individuals and the values gained from important others in that social environment (Sutherland, 1939).

Children usually learn behavior from their significant or intimate others. These are people whom they admire and enjoy being around. If their significant others do not like white people and feel that the system is racist and stacked unfavorably against blacks then the child will grow up feeling the same way. If a child grow up being told by his/her significant other that black people are lazy, dishonest, violent, sex maniacs, always wanting something for nothing, criminal etc. then these kid grows up believing this and it remains a part of their thought process sometimes throughout life. It is much easier to retain our thoughts, attitudes and beliefs about things or people than it is to change them.

Perception Of Young Inner City Black Males

William Julius Wilson's research of 179 firms in Chicago on their perception of inner city blacks produced striking results that reported that employers "considered inner city workers—especially young black males to be uneducated, unstable, uncooperative, and dishonest" (Wilson, 1996, p. 111).

Walter Reckless theorized that gangs provided a learning environment intensely focused on male qualities and abilities admired in lower-class communities: toughness, street smartness, fighting ability, defeating rival groups by force and craft, earning respect by courage, and risk taking. He believed that criminal activity provided a means of attaining these goals (Miller, 1958:19).

According to Skinner (1971:16), behavior is shaped and maintained by its consequences. Therefore, behavior is a product of present and past events in the life of the individual. The contingencies of reinforcement and punishment (aversive

161

stimuli) determine whether the frequency of any particular behavior is increased or diminished.

C. Ray Jeffery suggest in his differential reinforcement theory that a stimulus will be more or less reinforcing depending on the individual's current condition. For example, a person who already have wealth (satiated) will be less likely to find robbing someone of their money to be reinforcing, while the impoverished individual (deprived) will more likely see the money as a rein forcer (Jeffery, 1965:295).

Economics As a Factor Of Crime and Delinquency

The economic status and conditions of individuals has in the past and will in the future continue to play a significant role in deciding who will become criminal.

One cannot deny the fact that jails and prisons are full of poor people. Many theorists jump on the bandwagon stating that minorities commit most of the crimes and that is why their numbers are as such in the correctional institutions. In this present age, we must be concerned about any research that make statements about the correctional system and not mention the effects of classism, poverty and racism on crime especially research that is race specific and include policy recommendation.

In the present and future, criminologists of color must not sit by and become hoodwinked by old research and old research methods that support the specific aim of certain criminologists on race, class and gender specific journeys to find research that will support their theory. Instead, they must conduct new research and report the findings in an unbiased manner whether it supports or disputes their theory.

Pitfalls of Bias Criminal Data

Young and Sulton (1991) noted female African American Criminologists, argues that African American criminologists generally are frustrated by their white counterpart's insistence on using available crime data to show that African Americans are disproportionately involved in crime. These criminologists argued that it is unprofessional to make such an allegation because the concept of disproportionality as employed by many white criminologists, is based on the groundless assumption that the contribution of African Americans to the total population should somehow influence their contribution in other areas. Completely ignored by these white criminologists is the qualifier: "all things being equal" Totally disregarded is the fact that all things are not equal. And masterfully understated is the fact that the vast majority of African Americans are not involved in any type of crime (1991, pp. 104-105).

Enviroecogenetics and Reality of Crime

One cannot argue with the fact that minorities commit more crimes in relations to their proportion in society, but one could argue that low socio-economic status, unstable and indecent employment, to a great extent is responsible for much of the crime in the black community. People in impoverished ghettoes and urban closets sweltering with the heat of injustice, exploitation and oppression grow weary of their lot in life.

People with nothing or very little to lose will often times take greater risk when it comes to criminal behavior. When you have nothing to lose, what's the big deal about getting caught?

Luxuries Of Perceived Economic Stability in Prison (Prison Princes)

Some people in prison live better than many of the people on the streets. In prison you have three hot meals and a bed, many inmates have cable T.V., heat in the winter and sometimes air in the summer, your utilities stay on, You do not have to worry about bill collectors bothering you, you have access to a telephone, controlled monitored visits, you are sober and usually get your proper amount of rest etc., that is much better than some people on the streets. Many people fail to realize that the Pauper-Prince-Pauper Syndrome affects the mentality of the prisoner. While on the street struggling the inmate is a pauper. In prison he has food service, warm bed, friends, healthy living environment, telephone, cable etc these luxuries allow his transformation into a Prince. When he is released and must give up these luxuries he reverts back to a Pauper in very many instances because society will not give him a job, his parole off will not give him a break, his family will not give him a chance and his only option to work comes from friends who are willing to employ him in the drug business. His options become to sell drugs and go back to jail or struggle in the streets hoping and praying that something miraculous happen and you are able to beat the odds.

Economic Status and its Impact On Crime

When people have good jobs, and decent income their accountability also increases these people are able to buy nice homes, cars and most of all they are able to pay their bills. When these kinds of conditions exist the likelihood of committing a crime or engaging in criminal conduct decreases significantly. There are masses of black people in the inner and outer city who cannot find employment.

The government continues to give fatalistic hope to the masses of poor and exploited people year after year, promising welfare to work programs and work training seminars that look good and sound good, but has no substance nor depth. In American Society the U.S. Government continues to reduce the food stamps, AFDC, WIC, Insurance, Subsidized Housing etc rolls. America's poor are constantly promised that they will be trained and placed in positions of employment. Many of these people who complete these training seminars are given jobs at places such as McDonalds, Burger King, Merry Maids etc.

Harms of Welfare Reform and its Affect On Crime

In the U.S. Government's eyesight they have just removed a person off the welfare role and assisted them in finding decent employment. This scenario is not found to be worthy of praise by many people who know that these kinds of decisions will come back to haunt the government and the people on welfare

165

affected with these decisions. Most of these people are in worst shape after they begin to work than they were when they received assistance from the government. Most of these jobs do not provide insurance for these parents nor their children neither do they provide full-time employment. In these back to work programs, the government will take one or two people and put them into a decent job and make them poster children, when the remaining masses of trainees remain unemployed or underemployed.

It would be hard to argue and disagree with the system if the system provided decent employment to those who wanted to work, but they don't. If crime rates are to change, economic conditions must change.

The Reality of Being Unemployed or Underemployed

Research and situational-conditions have shown that if for some reason the rich and wealthy citizens of America became poor, for the most part they would become criminals also which illustrates that enviroecogenetics has a great impact on crime and delinquency. Edwin Sutherland according to Williams and McShane (1998), said that during the depression while serving with the Bureau of Hygiene in New York, he saw people who had not been criminal, nor associated with criminals, commit criminal acts as a direct result of their impoverished situations during the depression (Williams, McShane, 1998).

Questionable Conclusions

When criminologists allude to the fact that many of the poor never commit crimes and therefore there is no strong correlation between crime and poverty they are referring to a special population. Research findings such as this is welcomed in big government politics and policy reform because it allows the government to not have to fix the poverty problem, nor put much emphasis on this strongest factor associated with crime.

Enviroecogenetics and Marxism

Karl Marx said that there was an ongoing conflict with the rich and the poor and that the rich controlled the means of production and the power to lobby for enactment of laws that would benefit his interest, while at the same time keeping the poor in an impoverished state. According to Marx, the capitalist society is structured to keep the rich in power and the poor in poverty. Until the poor realize that the rich and wealthy citizens of this country needs them to make their surplus profits, The rich and wealthy will continue to exploit the poor and lower classes with low wages and long hours.

Black Criminologist's View On Crime And Poverty

W.E.B. Dubois said, " We must remember that crime is not normal; that the appearance of crime among Southern Negroes is a symptom of wrong social conditions-of a stress of life greater than a large part of the community can bear. The Negro is not naturally criminal; he is usually patient and law abiding--- We must look for remedy in the sane reform of these wrong social conditions, and not in intimidation, savagery, or in the

167

legalized slavery of men (Du Bois, 1901a/1982, p.116). Du Bois when on to say concerning the large black prison population in the North, "What else is this but a logical result of bad homes, poor health, restricted opportunities for work, and general social oppression? —That the Negro under normal conditions is law-abiding and good-natured cannot be disputed. We have but to change conditions, then to reduce Negro crime. (Du Bois, 1901b, p.15).

Monroe Work (1900) researched black crime in Chicago and concluded that Negroes in Chicago were in a poorer economic condition, which accounted for their excess of crime (ibid. p. 223).

Coramae R. Mann in the publication Sister against Sister, concluded through her research that in reference to female on female crime the offenders tend to be predominantly black, undereducated, unemployed, have prior arrest records and commit their offenses in residences (Mann, 1993a, p. 202). Poverty is a recurring factor that is associated with crime at every significant level throughout the system. Further research indicated that joblessness and poverty appear to exert much influence on violent crime (murder and robbery) indirectly through family disruption [i.e.. female headed households] p.40. And that the conditions that whites and blacks live in are remarkably different "especially with regard to concentrated urban poverty" p.41 (Sampson, Wilson, 1995).

Darnell Hawkins, in his third proposition explaining a causal model of black homicide suggested, " economic deprivation creates a climate of powerlessness in which individual acts of violence are likely to take place, and that an adequate theory of black violence must explore the direct link between present day African American disadvantage and violent crime" (1983, p. 125). This proposition taken from (Fanon, 1952,1963) has been resurrected by Staples (1974) and Tatum (1994).

Genetics' Impact On Crime

Many Theorists in the pass have concluded that criminality is inherited. A Physiognomist of the sixteenth century, J. Baptiste Della Porte, Related characteristics of the body to criminality (Schafer, 1976:38). In the early 1800's Phrenologists Franz Gall and Johann Gaspar Spurzheim, believed that the characteristics of the brain are mirrored in bumps on the skull. During the middle of the nineteenth century Lombroso, Criminal Man (1863); Garafalo, Criminology (1885); and Ferri, Criminal Sociology (1884), concluded that some people have biological and mental traits that make them crime prone. These traits they believed were inherited and present at birth. Mental and Physical degeneracy was thought to be the primary causes of crime (Siegel, 1995). Cloninger et al (1982) examined children whose biological parents were criminals, crime rate for children were 4 times greater if biological parents were criminals, 2 times greater if adopted parents were criminals. Research such as this cannot be disputed. There is a link between children of

169

parents that are criminal. It is the assumption of enviroecogentics that genetics does play a role in a person's propensity to commit crime. However, all people are susceptible to these criminal tendencies. Just as some children are predisposed to a greater extent to become alcoholics, develop hypertension, glaucoma, sickle cell, various cancers etc, some children are more prone to becoming criminals. This predisposition is determined by the child's environment, economic status and genetic predisposition.

Later in life Lombroso also acknowledged that social and economic conditions were factors that influenced crime. However, he insisted that these causes were secondary in nature to biological factors.

Richard Dugdale's study of six generations of the Juke family was used to infer that criminal (and antisocial) behavior is inherited (Dugdale, 1877). Other hereditary factors were considered through the examination of twins (Lange, 1919), general body types (Krfetschmer, 1926; Hooten, 1939; Sheldon, 1949; Glueck and Glueck, 1950), and even endocrinology (Schlapp and Smith, 1928). Other Theorist such as Mednick (1977, 1987), Jeffery, (1989), and Herrnstein (1985), assumes that genes directly or indirectly affect criminal behavior.

Automation, Slavery, Convict-Lease System and Modern Prison Populations.

Because crime is associated with being black, one can theorize that the warehousing of hundreds of thousands of black inmates may be one of the greatest acts of eugenics (population control) in the world. This form of eugenics (imprisonment) may be used exclusively to keep blacks from the ballot boxes in large numbers. Prior to automation and during slavery, black muscle was needed to pick cotton and work in factories in the northern U.S., but at the turn of the century during the industrialization of America machines (combines, tractors) and advanced technology replaced muscle labor with machine labor creating less dependency on black labor to produce surplus profits. This surplus labor as Marx referred to the unemployed was no longer needed. It was after the civil war that the convict lease system became popular. The convict lease system returned blacks to the plantations via the jailhouses in the south. Blacks were confined to jails in alarming rates for vagrancy laws and failing to pay their poll taxes. Today over one million black men are locked up in America's jails and prisons. The majorities of them (60-80%) are confined for drug or drug related offenses.

As blacks remain warehoused in jails and prisons the black population fades tremendously. Is this a coincidence? Or is this subtle-specific-strategic planning? If these surplus laborers were not locked up the African American population would increase substantially. Every baby born represents a vote and in a democracy a substantial increase in voting power means an increase in threats to those in power (Blalock, 1967).

Society is structured in such a way as to keep the rich in power and the poor continuously depending on the rich. The fact that

171

ex-felons cannot vote is very important to those in power. Felon voting rights can and would determine outcomes in many elections and therefore is considered a threat to the power structure.

Genetics and its relationship to crime

Unlike early Positivist Theorist, Enviroecogenetics does not theorize nor believe that criminals can be identified by external characteristics. However, like Richard Dugdale (1877), Enviroecogenetics, theorizes that people who come from parents that have been convicted of crimes and have been labeled as criminal are predisposed to a greater extent to become delinquent or criminal for several reasons:

Most ex-convicts find fault with the justice system and internalize the structure and system as being bias, prejudice and against them, this attitude is transmitted through family transmission from parent(s) to child/children causing innocent children to develop a displeasure for the law and the legal justice system. Research has indicated that children who come from families in which their biological parents were convicted criminals are four times more likely to become criminals and adopted children who come from homes in which one or more parent(s) is a convicted criminal are two times more likely to engage in criminal conduct. Analysis of the family histories of inmates, and ex-felons indicates that previous family members have been associated with crime in most cases and depending on their age, if older, their off springs are associated with crime.

Enviroecogenetics argues that criminals are not born. They are however, evolutionized through interactions brought on by environmental exposures coupled with economics depravations and genetic predispositions.

Enviroecogenetics Theory Analysis and Critique

Many Criminologists and Sociologists have researched and published opinions and theories explaining causal explanations of crime and delinquency in society. Analyzing many of these theories, it comes as no surprise that many theorists and researchers have failed to identify economics as a major factor associated with crime. Economics according to enviroecogenetics is the major factor associated with delinquency and crime.

One does not have to be a rocket Scientist or Criminologist to recognize that the poor is represented in the majority at every phase of the criminal justice system process in every state in America.

Proportionately the majority of prisoners and detainees are poor and non-white based on proportion to population. Disproportionality is evident throughout the criminal justice system. People who are poor, live in bad environments and are off springs of criminals are very much more likely to be incarcerated than the middle-class or wealthy citizens of society.

Stress, Strain and Black Imprisonment

Emile Durkheim introduced the concept of Anomie in his book *The Division of Labor in Society,* in 1893. He used *Anomie* to describe a condition of deregulation that was occurring in society. This meant that rules on how people ought to behave with each other were breaking down and they no longer knew what to expect from each other. This concept was explained by analyzing the mass influx of immigrants who migrated to America in the 1800's and the early 1900's during the industrial revolution. As immigrants came to America they bought with them their particular cultures, norms, languages and customs and as America became greatly diversified normlessness or anomie became more prevalent. Anomie, simply defined, is a state where norms (expectations and behaviors) are confused, unclear or not present.

Durkheim felt that this normlessness led to deviant behavior. In his book *Division of Labor,* Durkheim proposed that societies evolved from a simple, non-specialized form, called mechanical. In this type of society people thought alike and performed basically the same kinds of work. This included agrarian societies that lived on agriculture. Most farmers planted the same crops and harvested crops the same and used the same terminology. Secondly, Durkheim proposed that mechanical societies evolved to a highly complex, specialized form that he referred to as organic. He believed that as societies became more complex or organic that the breakdown in communication occurred and people no longer were tied together and social bonds became impersonal (Durkheim, 1893).

Robert K. Merton borrowed Durkheim's concept of anomie and developed his own theory, called *Strain Theory*. Merton argued that the real problem is not created by a sudden change as Durkheim had suggested, but rather by a social structure that holds out the same goals to all of its members without giving them equal means to achieve them. Merton believed that it was this lack of integration between what the culture called for and what the structure permits (*Differential Opportunity Theory overlap*) that cause deviant behavior.

Merton emphasized that there are certain goals that are strongly sought after by society and that society emphasized certain means in which to attain these goals such as (education, hard work, etc.,) But he suggested that not everyone has equal access to the legitimate means to attain these goals. As a result of this stage, anomie becomes present (Merton, 1938).

Many citizens in America are quick to say that we all have the same opportunities. This statement may hold some truth and may be generalized to the vast segment of the population. However, when analyzed in light of strain theory, one quickly conclude that Merton is not arguing the fact that everyone has access to legitimate means to attain the goals of society. Merton is arguing the fact that these opportunities are not equal. Most families see commercials and advertisement that suggest that they live in certain places and possess certain things, namely that they own a piece of America. This is part of the American dream. Americans should own their own home and two automobiles. Americans should have money saved to send their children to college. Americans should take a vacation at least once a year. Americans should be able to take their families to athletic events and etc. All of these things are great and most families that can afford these types of activities will follow the status quo. *Enviroecogenetics* would argue in agreement with Merton that there are some factors that must be taken into consideration that leads to strain.

Enviroecogenetics would first of all suggest that everyone is not born equal. Some people are born in hospitals and tended to by trained medical doctors that examine them and ensure their health, while some extremely poor persons are born at home to midwives who's only job is to deliver the baby. These people are not trained to treat illnesses.

Some children are born to rich and middle-class parents who are well educated and can afford to hire professionals to prepare their children to have competitive edges in their quest to attain their goals in life. Some children are born to very poor parents who are extremely uneducated or undereducated and can barely keep their bills paid.

Agreeing with Merton these children of the poor start out at a disadvantage. Merton suggested that there were five modes of adaptation that individuals chose in adapting to the strain caused by their restricted access to socially approved goals and means. He did not mean that everyone who was denied access to society's goals became deviant, but he suggested that their modes of adaptation would depend on how they viewed the cultural goals and the institutional means to achieve those goals. Merton believed that conformity was the most common mode of adaptation.

This was when individuals accepted the goals and the means to achieve them. The conformist would be the people who work the nine to five and live within his/her means.

The innovators are the persons that accept the goals of American society but designed their own means to get them.

Innovators include those people who see the new Lexus Coupe advertised, apply for the high paying jobs to get one, but is repeatedly turned down for various reasons including lack of education, skills, training, prior felony, lack of experience etc. Soon these people become frustrated and give up on the legitimate means and innovate (design) other ways to attain their goal through unconventional means. This may include embezzlement, robbery or other such criminal acts.

The ritualist is the individual that abandon the goals they once believed in and thought were within their reach and dedicate themselves to their current

Lifestyles.

The retreatists are people who give up on the goals and the means and retreat to the world of alcoholism and drug addition. These people become unproductive and non-striving.

In this respect Enviroecogenetics would identify many of the homeless, panhandlers, tree-dwellers (refers to the many people who gather under trees in the urban communities to drink wine, whiskey and beer from sun up to sun down on a daily basis) as retreatists.

Merton's fifth mode of adaptation is rebellion. Individuals who become rebellious create their own goals and their own means, by protest or revolutionary activity. Groups like *Move*, Ramona Africa, Huey Newton and Bobby Seale of the Black Panthers, David Koresh and the Davidian Cult,

And David Duke and the *Imperial Knights of the Klu Klux Klan* would be identified as rebellious groups according to (Merton, 1938).

Revisiting Power Threat Theory

Tracy Andrus

Power threat theory dates to 1967 and was first introduced by Hubert Blalock. Blalock (1967) theorized that when one group threatens the existence or order of a group or community as a whole the result would be excommunication, eradication or both.

Power threat is generally described as the actual or perceived potential of a minority group to pose a realistic challenge to white political or economic control. Blalock proposes that the power threat factor should predominate three areas of prejudice or discrimination:

1. **Restriction of a minority's political rights.**

2. **Symbolic forms of segregation.**

3. **A threat-oriented ideological system**.

Some criminological research suggests that the disproportionate processing of blacks within the criminal justice system likely reflects elements of each of these areas of discrimination such as political participation (Heer 1959; Key 1949), income (Blalock 1956, 1957: Frisbie and Neidert 1977), occupational status (Glenn 1963, 1964), school desegregation (Pettigrew 1957), lynching (Corzine et al. 1983), police strength (Jacobs, 1979; Carroll, 1981; and Liska et al, 1981, 1985).

A series of studies link the size of the nonwhite population, race relations, and police strength. Jacobs reports that metropolitan areas with larger numbers of blacks had stronger law enforcement agencies than areas with fewer blacks in 1970 but not in 1960. Jackson and Carroll (1981) concluded that police expenditures are a resource that is mobilized or expanded when a minority group appears threatening to the dominant group. Liska et al. (1985) provides additional support for the significance of power threat factors

In the social control of blacks. Liska et al (1985) supports the hypothesis that a high percentage of nonwhites and a low level of segregation increase the perceived threat of crime. Power threat considerations may also be useful for explaining black-white punishment differences across crime types. Some crimes may be seen as being more threatening to white authority than others. A racial power threat can be hypothesized to influence the behavior of not only the police themselves but also various other government officials. Hence, prosecutors, judges, correctional officials and others should be similarly affected and likely to produce similar race-related outcomes.

This theory is based on the premise that if minority groups would organize and pull together in a cohesive manner they would be in a position to challenge or gain political dominance and/or rise to a level in which they may compete with the dominant group. Power threat theory specifies that, as the percentages of blacks or minorities increase, the chance to dominate increases also. The majority group's motivation to discriminate is a function of two types of perceived threats, economic and political (competition and power), and that both are related to minority proportion but in different ways. Blalock hypothesizes that when discrimination is motivated by threats of competition, research would discover a nonlinear relationship with a decreasing slope; when the motivation is a product of power threats, the expected relationship will be nonlinear with an increasing slope.

Blalock believed that when the majority population was confronted with economic or political threats mechanisms had to be put in place to maintain dominance for the majority population. An example of this would be the post civil war black codes and vagrant laws that were purposely introduced to prohibit blacks from gaining political and economic power. These laws put the power of the plantation owner into the hands of the state, the state became the new taskmaster and the law was the leverage that was used to help the state maintain the status quo of the day.

The formation of the modern state became necessary with the development of capitalism because the economy was based on the exploitation of one class by another, therefore a political class was needed that would perpetuate that order (Cullen and Agnew, 1999). The state thus arose to protect and promote the interests of the dominant class. The state exists as a device for controlling the exploited class, the class that labors for the benefit of the ruling class (Cullen and Agnew, 1999). Criminal law developed as the most appropriate form of control for capitalist society (Cullen and Agnew, 1999).

According to Blalock, power threat theory theorizes that African Americans are the recipients of retributive justice that serves to keep them from the ballot box. The ballot box is the most powerful tool used to maintain the status quo in America. There are offenses committed by the government against persons and groups who would seemingly threaten national security (Cullen and Agnew, 1999). Included here are the crimes of warfare and political assassination of foreign and domestic leaders (Cullen and Agnew, 1999). Therefore,

181

powerbrokers and lawmakers create laws to maintain the leverage of power that has been maintained throughout the history of America   Drawing primarily on the works of Hubert Blalock (1967), Hawkins believed that the notion of a power threat theory is potentially applicable to conflict theory. Hawkins describe the power threat hypothesis as:

The actual or perceived potential of a minority group to pose a realistic challenge to white political or economic control will cause a reaction. Hawkins believes that power-threat should predominate in three areas: (1) restriction of minority's political rights, (2) symbolic forms of segregation, and (3) a threat-oriented ideological system. (1987, p. 735). Hawkins suggests that some research supports his contention that the above areas of discrimination are possibly linked to the overrepresentation of African Americans within the criminal justice system (pp. 735-36). Many theorists assume that as long as the percentages of minorities remain constant and do not increase to such a level that they may cause concern for the dominant group there will be no reaction from the dominant group and the level of prejudice and racism will ultimately remain low. According to Blalock (1967), those in power will create mechanisms beforehand that may be used to control the minority population should that group begin to pose a threat to the status quo. Those mechanisms include subtle laws and ordinances.

A large minority percentage may not produce a power threat unless there is a clear-cut distinction between the minority and the dominant group (Blalock, 1967). Blalock believed that the Irish, Poles and Italians were able to assimilate much better than blacks in America because there were fewer obvious distinctions. Blalock believed that an increase in minority percentages would result in an increase in discrimination because of heightened perceived competition, an increased power threat and because members of the dominant group would use political means to achieve economic ends, or vice versa.

Power threat differs from other conflict theories in that it hypothesizes that those trying to maintain control are held together because of race or natural origin, whereas conflict theorists believe that those in power use their wealth to create laws to maintain the status quo. In the power threat perspective violence is used in addition to the creation of laws to maintain control, whereas violence is not viewed as a mechanism of control used by those desiring to maintain control in the conflict structure. The conflict perspective differs from power threat in that it views the struggle as being between the haves and the have-nots disregarding race. Power threat views the struggle as being between the majority and the minority where race and national origin is inclusive.

The effect of the relative size of a minority group on discriminatory actions by the majority has been a major problem in studies of inter-group relations dating back to the early 1950s. While examining the effect of percent black on racial differences in unemployment and occupational status in 90 U.S. cities, (Turner, 1951), found limited support for the view that minority proportion is directly related to the level of discrimination, a proposition first advanced by (Williams, 1947). Subsequent studies showed percent black to be positively related to diverse measures of discrimination, including socioeconomic inequality (Blalock, 1956, 1957; Glen, 1964), school segregation (Pettigrew, 1957), black voter registration rates (Matthews and Prothro, 1963; Price, 1957), and support for white supremacy candidates (Heer, 1959).

Although several studies following Blalock have reported percent minority to be directly related to forms of discrimination (Brown and Fuguitt, 1972; Frisbie and Neidert, 1977; Jibou and Marshall, 1971; Reed, 1972; Vanfossen, 1968; Wasserman and Segal, 1973; Wilcox and Roof, 1978), there are two systematic variations in the findings. First, for measures of economic inequality, the correlations are stronger and more consistent for education and income than for occupation. Secondly, (Glenn, 1964), suggests that where blacks comprise a large percentage of the population, they overflow into better occupations, satisfying a labor force need and attenuating the effects of discrimination. This overflow hypothesis is supported by (Wilcox and Roof, 1978).

The Historical Context Of Competition And Perceived Power Threat

Throughout the history of America Anglos have dehumanized minorities in the United States in one sense or another. Anglos of the United States have always remained united when power and control were at issue. Any attempt by a minority class to adjust or use

the American capitalist system has usually been met with sudden destruction and fervor. The criminal justice system of the United States has always served the interests, and been the defender of, the existing social orders. The criminal system has been viewed as a mechanism used to process poor and minority offenders. Many of these offenders could find no meaningful place in the labor market. While ignoring the illegalities of the rich and powerful corporate offenders until they are forced to deal with them because of public confrontation or as a result of a whistle blowing. Jeffery Reiman's title to his book seems to fit appropriately here because the system is viewed by the poor as being designed in such a manner in which the "rich get richer and the poor get prison" (Reiman, 1984).

In the south, Lewis Copeland pointed out that the Negro was often seen in sharp contrast to whites. Copeland said many southern whites glorified the "old-time darky", the "Uncle Tom" and "mammy" figures of southern tradition. This image was in sharp contrast to the "uppity nigger" and the "militant Yankee Negro". The first type is completely non-threatening and serves to bring forth paternalistic feelings of tenderness toward the childlike Negro. The second image calls for intense hatred and fear.

Historical Evidence of Power Threat: Past to Present
Penal Evidence

Like the Black Codes, Vagrancy laws, and sharecropping arrangements, the convict lease system was a mechanism of race control used to prevent ex-slaves from obtaining the status and rights enjoyed by wageworkers. The organization and philosophy of crime control both before and after the Civil War reflected the fact that both slaves and ex-slaves were problem populations. As such, they were a threat to the existing system of class rule but also a useful resource. Economically they were viewed as a pool of cheap labor for industrialization, and politically or symbolically as a means to consolidate white supremacy.

These principles date back to the post Civil War era and are clearly implicated in the rise of black imprisonment following the Civil War, which illustrates the distinctive racial dynamics in operation as shown by (Rusche and Kirchheimer, 1968/1939).

After the Civil War blacks were viewed as threatening to the white power structure because millions of blacks were suddenly transformed from personal property to potential competitors (Tolnay and Beck 1995, p.57). After the Civil War whites competed with blacks for jobs. Plantation owners competed with one another in the form of higher wages for good help. In addition, many whites feared domination by newly freed blacks (Oshinsky 1996, p. 19). In order to maintain control over the newly released slave and prevent him from becoming a threat to the white power structure the convict lease system was formed. This allowed plantation owners to hire cheap labor and regain control. The threat of plantation prisons kept many blacks in servitude under labor contracts that re-created the conditions of slavery (Gorman 1997, p.450).

Adamson (1983,1984) argued that immediate post-civil War social control of blacks by criminal justice systems in the south reflected the fact that blacks were both potential threats to white control and potential assets (prison labor).

To understand the political and economic forces which shaped the post-civil War approach to crime control and punishment, it is necessary to keep in mind that plantation justice tended to siphon blacks out of the state punishment system in the pre-civil war period. Slaves were punished according to slave codes the criminal justice system, which emerged prior to the Civil war, was for whites only.

Slaves freed legally by the 13th amendment in 1865 were both a threat to social relations and a useful resource, a dangerous population, which stood in need of control but also a welcome source of manpower. The fact that the emancipated slaves represented both a dangerous class and, in the words Marx used to describe the reserve army of labor, "a mass of

187

human material always ready for exploitation" (Marx, 1967:631), helps to explain the rise of the convict lease system.

Like monarchial law, the slave codes prescribed barbaric and public punishments. The heads of 16 rebels in Louisiana were "stuck upon poles along the Mississippi River as a grim warning to other slaves" (Stampp, 1956:135). The northern prison reformer, Matthew Carey, was sickened to learn that South Carolina had enacted a law "for burning alive slaves who murdered their masters" (Carey, 1831:12). By turning punishment into a public spectacle, rulers were able to legitimate an absolute control over their subjects (Foucault, 1977). Plantation slaves were made to witness the awesome force of their white masters at public hangings and whippings.

The 13th and 14th amendments to the U.S. Constitution ratified by congress in 1865 and 1868 created a new class of offenders. Blacks, who comprised more than 50% of the population of Louisiana, Mississippi, and South Carolina, were now to be punished as free men (Carleton, 1971:44). Although the republicans who had taken over the instruments of governments in the confederate states by 1867 promised fair trials and equal treatment for black defendants and prisoners were acknowledged de jure, these rights could not be recognized de facto, without posing a challenge to the economic superiority of the white race. During 1867 the radical republicans introduced the black codes. More than vagrancy laws, their purpose was to keep the Negro exactly what he was:

a property-less rural laborer under strict controls, without political rights, and with inferior legal rights" (Stampp, 1965:79).

In one county in Georgia, officials sentenced blacks to long stretches of hard labor for what amounted to improper demeanor spitting, swearing and trespassing (Novak, 1978:35). County courts were virtually employment bureaus. Company agents traveled from county court to county court to pick up men and women. Often offenders who had worked off their debt were arrested while returning home, prosecuted as vagrants, and returned for another stint of unpaid toil (Carter, 1964:95).

Democrats in Mississippi secured passage of that state's "pig" law, which defined the theft of property worth more than $10.00 including cattle and swine as grand larceny, punishable by up to five years of hard labor (Wharton, 1965:237). In 1875 a similar law in Georgia made stealing hogs a felony. North Carolina courts did not distinguish between petty and grand larceny, so that a person could get three to 10 years for stealing a couple of chickens (Logan, 1964:193).

Racial Redistricting and Realignment

Racial redistricting emerged as one of the most fiercely debated policy questions among scholars, judges, and politicians during the 1990s. The empirical contentions revolve around the policy's partisan impact. Political scientist have criticized racial redistricting by claiming that packing black voters into majority-minority districts cripples the democratic party outside of the safe seats it creates for black representatives (e.g., Bullock 1995; Lublin 1997; Lublin and Voss 1998; Swain 1995a, 1995b; Thernstorm and Thernstrom 1997). Research on racial redistricting in 10 southern states suggest that racial redistricting systematically harms the party chosen by most black voters, as critics contend. The new black redistricting districts cost the Democratic Party legislative seats in all ten states and likely accounted for the Democrats losing control of the state houses in both South Carolina and Virginia for the first time since Reconstruction.

African Americans voters strongly support the Democratic Party. White southerners, by contrast, display a strain of political conservatism that has been funneling them toward the GOP. Since racial redistricting pulls black voters into majority-minority enclaves, and must do so in the bounds of similarly situated legislative districts, it naturally strips an overwhelmingly loyal democratic voting base out of surrounding constituencies and replaces them with white who usually exhibit no such fidelity. Common sense would seem to dictate that redistricting must hurt the south's Democrats (Epstein and O'Halloran 1999, 388).

White voters who reside in a mixed neighborhood exist in an integrated social and economic world that other whites do not share. Proximity may spur competition between races and expand the opportunity for negative interracial contact-spawning an antipathy ripe for political exploitation (Brewer and Miller 1984, 291-295). Integrated whites inclined to act against this power threat in their neighborhood would rally behind the racially conservative Republican Party, hoping for policies that would give them the upper hand in any inter-group conflict (Huckfeldt and Kohfeld 1989, 80-83).

Black Codes and Vagrancy Laws

Whites reduced the threat of losing power to blacks by arresting blacks based on the Slave Codes of 1865-1866 and later resurrected the same codes during the period of 1877 and beyond (Gorman 1997, p. 447). When the police spotted able-bodied black men they were arrested and charged with crimes they had not committed. When these men could not pay their fines they were forced to go to work (Gorman, 1997). Bogus arrests were sometimes orchestrated by employers working hand-in-glove with local officials to keep their work camps well stocked with able-bodied blacks (Oshinsky 1996, p. 71).

When viewing the power threat hypothesis, the picture that emerges is of black convicts as slaves and the state functioning as slave master (Gorman 1997). Hawkins describes black criminality at this juncture as being less the product of the conduct of blacks and more dependent upon the social standing of blacks (Hawkins 1995, p. 34). Power threat has affected other minorities as well. For example, after the transcontinental railroad was completed, Asian labor was no longer needed. The surplus Asian labor threatened the fair wage of the average white American worker. To control this population, the U.S.

either passed laws that selectively prohibited "Orientals" from possessing drugs or selectively enforced drug laws against them (Barak, Flavin, Leighton, 2001).

It is believed that many American laws have been enacted with a specific intent to silence, weaken and discourage minorities in the United States (Lusane 1991, p.34). These laws were created and enacted with the particular purpose of reducing the political clout of those who threaten the status quo. A good example of this kind of practice would involve looking at the Chinese Exclusion Act of 1882. This act outlawed the importation of Chinese Opium that was primarily used by the Chinese (Williams, 2002). This law also outlawed opium use among Chinese but not whites (Lusane 1991, p.31). In 1937 the U.S. passed the Marijuana Tax Act that prevented Mexicans from harvesting marijuana for personal use and trafficking. These laws were created and enacted by the white male dominant culture groups of America. These laws have thus far succeeded in accomplishing the desired results of the dominant power structure by keeping the rich and powerful in influential positions to make decisions that protect and guard their power while reducing the power of threatening groups that may challenge the status quo.

The war on drugs that has been visible in America has really been a war on the poor and powerless and has resulted in the incarceration and disenfranchisement of millions of minorities. Jerome Miller has called this kind of policing the search and destroying of African American males (Miller, 1997). Even statues that are facially neutral can still have a disproportionate impact on minorities. The law may not be racist in its intent but is racist in its effect. As a case in point, the federal sentencing guidelines penalize the possession of crack cocaine more heavily than powdered cocaine in a 100 to 1 ratio. About 85 percent of those sent to prison under the crack provisions of this law are black, this pattern of sentencing contributes directly to problems of disproportionate minority confinement (Bureau of Justice Statistics 1997b).

According to the National Institute of Drug Abuse, 50 percent of crack users are white as compared to 36 percent black (Bureau of Justice Statistics 1992). Former Drug Czar William Bennett acknowledged that the typical crack smoker is a white suburbanite (Lusane 1991).

Purposeful Perpetuation Of Criminal Activity By The U.S. Government

The government employs millions of law enforcement agents, including border control officers, CIA, ATF, FBI, DEA, Office of National Drug Control and numerous other departments to protect and control the borders and boundaries of the U.S. Yet, drugs are available in almost every city and on almost every corner in the United States. Some researchers have suggested that America cannot afford to stop the influx of millions of tons of cocaine and other illegal drugs into the United States, because it would seriously handicap the criminal justice system. It is the belief of many people that the U.S. government, people who are employed by the criminal justice system and all other entities that depend on crime and criminal activity as a basis for employment cannot afford to stop or slow down the war on crime and drugs.

African Americans were the fastest growing minority for many years. Their threat to white America resulted in the convict lease system and the present day confinement of a large proportion of blacks for numerous reasons. Today, Hispanics are the fastest growing ethnic group in the United States and this group is expected to include one in every four Americans in 2050 (U.S. Census, 1997). It is theorized that their presence and threat at the ballot box has been factors that caused Hispanics to become the fastest growing population in prisons from 1980 to 1993 (Donziger, 1996:104).

If prisons were included in the nation's unemployment rate the rate would increase by 1.5% or more (Reiman, 1998). There are currently over two million people incarcerated in American prisons and jails today. Crime pays tremendous dividends for business interests and many companies are operating prisons for profits today. It is therefore logical that a business-friendly government will do whatever it takes to ensure a steady supply of offenders, so that the criminal justice system can continue to pay off (Christie, 1994).

Many studies have concluded that "law and order" policies that have been in place have rather than reducing crime and harms, contributed to the problems entailed in reducing crime and enhancing justice (Beckett and Sasson 2000; Cole 1999; Currie 1998; Lynch and Patterson 1991; Miller 1997; Reiman 1998a). Power threat theorists, as does most radical-conflict theorists identified patterns in which minorities have been removed from society in disproportionate numbers. Many criminologists and social scientists have

If prisons were included in the nation's unemployment rate the rate would increase by 1.5% or more (Reiman, 1998). There are currently over two million people incarcerated in American prisons and jails today. Crime pays tremendous dividends for business interests and many companies are operating prisons for profits today. It is therefore logical that a business-friendly government will do whatever it takes to ensure a steady supply of offenders, so that the criminal justice system can continue to pay off (Christie, 1994).

Many studies have concluded that "law and order" policies that have been in place have rather than reducing crime and harms, contributed to the problems entailed in reducing crime and enhancing justice (Beckett and Sasson 2000; Cole 1999; Currie 1998; Lynch and Patterson 1991; Miller 1997; Reiman 1998a). Power threat theorists, as does most radical-conflict theorists identified patterns in which minorities have been removed from society in disproportionate numbers. Many criminologists and social scientists have

If prisons were included in the nation's unemployment rate the rate would increase by 1.5% or more (Reiman, 1998). There are currently over two million people incarcerated in American prisons and jails today. Crime pays tremendous dividends for business interests and many companies are operating prisons for profits today. It is therefore logical that a business-friendly government will do whatever it takes to ensure a steady supply of offenders, so that the criminal justice system can continue to pay off (Christie, 1994).

Recent Laws

Codified laws have impacted minorities in every facet of life. Felony adjudications and convictions that rise from drug arrests have disproportionately affected African Americans and Hispanics despite data showing that Anglos have been arrested at a much larger percent.

Every year legislatures create and enact new laws that drastically target and affect minorities (Sasson and Beckett, 1999). Conservative Republicans are quick to point out that the majority of crimes that are committed are committed in the black or minority neighborhoods. What is not explained is the over-representation of police presence in minority neighborhoods. One study found that although African Americans make up about 17% of drivers and only 17.5% of traffic violators, they made up nearly 73% of those pulled over and searched by the police (Gaines et al., 2000). If police were present in middle and upper class neighborhoods to the extent that they are in minority neighborhoods, there would be an increase in crimes reported in those neighborhoods and a reduction in the amount of crimes reported in minority neighborhoods. When police use race as a proxy for risk, being young, African American, and male equals probable cause (Gaines, 1993).

Research has concluded that laws were used to control free blacks after emancipation. Researchers have hypotheses that many laws enacted today have been enacted for the specific; purpose of maintaining the status quo. It has been hypotheses that certain laws serve to restrict the increase of minority populations through latent effects. Prison can be viewed as one of the greatest acts of eugenics in the western hemisphere.

Laws that have affected welfare reform, the introduction of birth control pills and the incentives that have been offered to women who have finished school without becoming pregnant out of wedlock are abstract shadows of power threat in action.

Laws such as three strikes, mandatory minimum sentencing, and federal sentencing guidelines for crack vs. powder cocaine have served to increase the minority prison population.

According to (Smothers, 1995), the Department of Justice exhorted Congress to reject the commission's proposal to make the penalty of crack cocaine the same as that for powder cocaine. Power threat theorists would suggest that the incarceration of multitudes of African Americans and Hispanics dilutes their voting power. Research has

Suggested that under the new Federal Sentencing Guidelines, investigators observed that African Americans are more likely than whites, to be sentenced to prison and to receive longer sentences. Overall, African Americans are less likely to receive a disposition of probation only. They are also less likely than any other group to have their counts reduced or dismissed for certain crimes. Since the inception of the federal sentencing guidelines, minority representation in prison has grown substantially (Free, 1997).

Effects of Perceived Threats Today in America

The creators or forgers of most laws in America are wealthy politicians who have vested interest in capital outlay projects and other enterprises. The created is the laws that are enacted to maintain the status quo. These laws allow the creators to maintain the upper hand and maintain a balance that is well tilted in their favor. These laws that are created serve to exploit the have-nots, in most cases permanently baring them from obtaining enough wealth to compete with the upper classes. The cremated are those that are pulverized when they attempt to threaten or compete against those in power.

The Effects Of A Felony

Ex Felons are prevented from voting in certain states and jurisdictions permanently once they have committed a felony. They are also prevented from obtaining a student loan for college and various financial aids when they have been convicted of a charge of possession for certain drug charges.

They are prevented from living in government-subsidized housing projects when they have been convicted of certain drug offenses. They are prevented from working in most law enforcement jobs even when the job does not require them to possess a weapon. Ex-felons are prevented from running for political office even though we live in a democratic society where government is supposed to be of the people, by the people, for the people. Ex-felons are prevented from entering into any military department or armed forces. Ex-felons are prevented from working in many banks and lending institutions. Ex-felons are prevented from holding many federal jobs. Ex-felons are prevented from obtaining most state issued occupational licenses. Ex-felons are prevented from obtaining alcohol beverage licenses. Ex-felons are prevented from selling real estate or obtaining a real estate license. Ex-felons are prevented from obtaining almost all state issued licenses including hunting licenses.

Ex-felons are prevented from obtaining state issued builder's licenses. Ex-felons are prevented from opening finance companies and lending institutions.

The removal of young black males from their communities has depleted the supply of potential marriage partners for young black females. These social relations have legitimated and encouraged female- headed households, creating the types of family formations that have been linked with higher rates of crime and abuse (Currie 1985; Messner and Rosenfield 1994).

These trends in racial punishment have reinforced and exacerbated the impoverishments in which many of these households have been found entrenched (Barak, Flavin and Leighton, 2001).

About the Author

Tracy Andrus is a PhD student majoring in Juvenile Justice at Prairie View A& M University in Prairie View, Texas. He also holds a B.S. in Criminal Justice from Louisiana College, a M.A. in Criminal Justice from the University of Louisiana at Monroe and a Bachelor of Theology from Shreveport Bible College.

Tracy Andrus is a contributing author to Tavis Smiley's book Keeping The Faith which has been nominated for a NAACP Award. After graduation he plans on remaining in academia and becoming a researcher. He is an ordained Baptist Minister.